An Illustrated Guide to
Classroom Organization
It Can Be Done, K-6

NEW, REVISED EDITION

Dinah Zike, M.Ed.

© 1989, 2005 Dinah Zike
Dinah-Might Adventures, LP
P.O. Box 690328
San Antonio, TX. 78269-0328
www.dinah.com

A Letter From Dinah Zike

Dear Educators:

This book is a newly-revised, updated, and expanded edition of my *Classroom Organization* book I originally began compiling in 1980 and published in 1989. It is an illustrated guide designed to help teachers solve some of the many organizational problems that arise in a typical classroom, and it is specifically designed for classrooms that use my *Foldables*™. I reassure teachers that it is not the BIG problems that cause teacher burnout—those problems advance to the next grade! It is the small, daily problems that begin to irritate and annoy. Lost pencils, no paper, arguments over crayons, glue containers that will not open, and mounds of paperwork year after year cause teacher burnout and early retirement!

I offer you this challenge: Write your problems on index cards, and persistently search for ways to alleviate them. You will be amazed at how even the smallest organizational changes can lessen the stress of teaching. The very nature of teaching — the unique and mercurial mix of students, parents, and administrators, as well as ever-changing teaching situations — makes it almost impossible to alleviate 100% of the problems. But, if we can alleviate 80 - 90% of the problems, the learning environment becomes more organized and comfortable, and the classroom becomes more enjoyable for both the teacher and the student.

Finding ways to solve MY problems is how this book originally began. I know that the information herein will not solve all of your problems, but I hope some of my insights will be of help to you, or at least stimulate you to develop your own creative solutions.

For the Love of Learning,

Dinah Zike

Acknowledgements

A Very Special Thank You To....

....the administration, staff, teachers, and students of
Boerne Independent School District, Boerne, Texas, and
Windcrest Elementary, Northeast Independent School District,
San Antonio, Texas, for the use of their facilities for
many of the classroom photographs in this book.

....Wilmet McLin, for allowing me to adopt her second graders
at Windcrest Elementary, San Antonio I.S.D.,
set up her classroom, and test strategies.

....Pat and Luella Connelly and the staff of Creative Teaching Press
for donating educational products and visual aids.

.....Anderson-Shiro Independent School District, Anderson, Texas,
for photographs of one of the author's former classrooms
where many of these ideas began.

....Chris Holden, a great artist, teacher, and father.

.....Mindy Neidner, DMA Director of Product Development, for her usual
dedication and determination to make this the best book possible.

....My husband, Ignacio Salas-Humara, for photographs,
book design, layout, and patience with the author.

Dedication
This book is dedicated to teachers in schools around the world
who have taught me to be a better teacher.
Thank you.

In Memoriam
In memory of Earl Jordan, a wonderful editor and friend.
You touched many lives in your short time with us.

Information on Dinah Zike

Other books and materials by Dinah Zike

To order a free catalog or to order Dinah's books and materials:
- Phone 1-800-99DINAH
- Fax 1-210-698-0095
- Email orders@dinah.com
- Write Dinah-Might Adventures, LP, P.O. Box 690328
San Antonio, Texas 78269-0328

To see the complete catalog and order Dinah Zike's books and materials, visit our website:
- **www.dinah.com**

Books in Dinah Zike's Big Book series

- *Dinah Zike's Big Book of Science: Elementary*
- *Dinah Zike's Big Book of Science: Middle School & High School*
- *Dinah Zike's Big Book of Math: Elementary*
- *Dinah Zike's Big Book of Math: Middle School & High School*
- *Dinah Zike's Big Book of Social Studies: Elementary*
- *Dinah Zike's Big Book of United States History: Grades 5-12*
- *Dinah Zike's Big Book of World History: Grades 6-12*
- *Dinah Zike's Big Book of Texas History: Grades 4-7*
- *Dinah Zike's Big Book of Books: Grades K-5*
- *Dinah Zike's Big Book of Projects: Grades K-12*

Keynotes and workshops by Dinah Zike

For information on keynotes and workshops please contact:
- Cecile Stepman
- Phone 210-698-0123
- Email dma@dinah.com

Dinah Zike Teaching Academy and Hill Country Retreat

Dinah is currently organizing a new teacher training school. It will be named the Dinah Zike Teaching Academy and Hill Country Retreat. It will be opening in June 2006 in the picturesque, historic village of Comfort, Texas, in the middle of the beautiful and famous Texas Hill Country. For more information please contact by email or fax:
- Dr. Judi Youngers, Director
- Email dza@hctc.net
- Fax 830-995-5205

E-Group

Join Dinah Zike's E-Group at www.dinah.com to receive latest updates and information on workshops, new books, and news!

Foldables™ K-12

What Are *Foldables*™, And Why Use Them?

Dinah Zike is noted internationally as the developer and inventor of three-dimensional graphic organizers, also called "*Foldables*™." These student-made reading, writing, and information study aids often require the use of supplies such as scissors, glue, markers, and other graphic art aids that need to be stored and organized.

Even though the focus of this book is grades K-6, middle school and high school teachers who use *Foldables*™ will find parts of this book very helpful.

Look for *Dinah Zike's Foldables*™ in math, science, social studies, health, and foreign language elementary, middle school, and high school textbooks published by Glencoe McGraw-Hill (www.glencoe.com) and Macmillan McGraw-Hill (www.macmillan.com).

Dinah Zike's Foldables™ can also be found in Dinah's *Big Book* series of books, and at her website at www.dinah.com.

Table Of Contents

Supplies	8
Pencils	9
Ink Pens	13
Glue	14
Scissors	20
Crayons	22
Water Colors Washes	27
Paints	28
Markers & Colored Pencils	30
Overhead Projector Markers	31
Write Here, On The Table	33
Storing Supplies	34
Cereal Box Storage	35
Trash	36
Photographs For Identity	38
Classroom Jobs	39
Helper's Wheel	41
Job Descriptions & Training	42
Pledge To The Flag	45
Handwriting Tablets & Notebook Paper	47
Publishing Center	48
Publishing Center: Reproducibles	51
Publishing Center: Graphics	56
Publishing Center: Scratch Paper	59
Publishing Center: Templates	60
Pubblishing Center: Rubber Stamps & Punches	61
Student Response Boards	62
Magnetic Boxes	64
Study Cards & Flash Cards	65
Flash Card & Stationery Pockets	67
Classroom Work Baskets	68
Hanging Student Work	70
Grades	71
Portfolios: Assessment & Storage	73
File Folders: Assessment & Storage	75
Assessment: Averaging Grades	76
Assessment In General	77
Assessment Documentation	78
Computer Lists	79
Grouping Activities	80
Lining Up	84
Show & Share	85
Check It Out!	86
Pass It Around	90
Take A Look At This!	91

Table Of Contents

Everyone Works & Shares 93
Junk Box Art & Stress Release 94
Home Survey 95
Home Survey Form (Sample) 96
Communicating & Networking 97
Collect Effectively 98
Garage Sales & Fleamarkets 99
Want Ads 100
Neighborhood Scavenger Hunt 101
Getting Help 102
Fold-away Teaching Aids 105
Using Bulletin Boards 107
Permanent Bulletin Boards 108
Shaped Bulletin Boards 109
Cubicles & Display 112
Bulletin Boards *Using Dinah Zike's Foldables™* ... 111
Bulletin Boards: 2" Tape 117
Bulletin Boards: Letters 118
Bulletin Boards: Activities 120
Preserving Specimens 121
Displaying Student Work 122
Displays For Student Work *Using Dinah Zike's Foldables™* ... 127
Classroom Storage 128
Classroom Furniture 133
Room Dividers 135
Language Arts Notes & Ideas 136
Handwriting Table & Activity Center 138
Art Center 139
Science Lab 140
Science Center vs. Natural History Museum 141
Science Centers *Using Dinah Zike's Foldables™* ... 142
Weather Station 143
Library & Research Center 144
Library Organization 145
Map & Globe Center 146
Social Studies/Current Events *Using Dinah Zike's Foldables™* ... 147
Social Studies *Using Dinah Zike's Foldables™* 148
Math Center 149
Measurement Center 150
Computer Center 151
First Aid Center 152
Setting Up A Classroom 153
Unit Boxes 157

Supplies

I Love The Smell of New School Supplies In The Morning

For many students the most exciting aspect of going back to school is getting their new supplies: packets of clean paper, long pencils with unused erasers, unbroken crayons with sharp points, and full glue containers that flow freely!

Teachers also love new supplies! It is easy to tell whether a teacher is still excited about teaching or is "burned out" by observing the manner in which he/she walks down the school supply aisle of a store. If the teacher walks slowly and takes deep breaths, enjoying the sight and smell of new, clean, unused, brightly colored supplies, he/she still has the enthusiasm needed to teach the K-6 student. However, if the teacher passes down the aisle quickly without noticing the glorious array and aroma of the area, not looking to the right or left, it is too late: the fire is gone. That teacher is burned out!

Remember: Students love their new supplies. Allow children of all ages to keep their materials for at least the first few days of school.

It is important that students learn to accept responsibility for their own possessions. Begin this important life-skill lesson at the beginning of the school year utilizing student supplies. The following sections of this book will introduce ways in which you can help students develop this important life skill.

Pencils

Painless Pencils

The pencil is probably the greatest daily source of frustration in the classroom. However, there are simple techniques that can turn this point of frustration into a means of positive production.

IN-SCHOOL SUPPLY SALES
Many schools raise money by selling unusual or novelty pencils. I discourage this since these fancy pencils often contribute to student distractions and sometimes discipline problems. Plain yellow, made-in-U.S.A. pencils with a strong #2 lead, or small reams of notebook paper sell very well as substitute items.

Sometimes This Works

On the first day of school have a new, sharpened pencil on each desk for each student. (Local businesses that use pencils for advertising are good sources for obtaining free pencils.) You have now started each student on an equal basis. The student is responsible for maintaining this pencil in good condition. Chewing, scissor carving, or any other form of mutilation is not allowed. Students are taught how to kindly "police" this rule (see page 11) and remind other students to take care of their pencils since others may have to use them later.

Plan Ahead as a Campus or District. When posting supply lists, request/require that students bring plain #2 pencils. Collect these pencils from students the first day of school. Pencils can become community property if they are generic.

Use unusual or special pencils, brought to the classroom from home or purchased in the school store, in learning stations or publishing centers. If students do not wish to place these pencils in special areas to be used by the class, they are asked to take them home to use for homework.

Pencils

Pencil Exchange

Have two pencil holders at the Supply Station. One container holds sharpened pencils, and the other is for "trade-in" pencils that wear down or break during class time. Students can exchange their dull or broken pencils during the day.

Electric or battery operated sharpeners are fast and efficient to use. To prevent waste, teach your Pencil Helper (see page 43) and individual students my "1-2-3" method of sharpening. Place the pencil in the sharpener, sharpen to the count of three, remove pencil, and check sharpness.

One count of three will sharpen dull pencils, and two or more counts of three will sharpen a broken pencil. The entire class will "hear" the amount of grinding noise made by the sharpener, thus policing its use.

Rule: No one can sharpen a pencil during instructional time. If possible, do not allow pencils to be taken from the classroom. (See page 12 for storage techniques.)

Only the Pencil Helper has permission to use the pencil sharpener, and then only at specified times (before class, during recess, etc.). Establish a short time each day for students to line up and have their pencils sharpened by the Pencil Helper. Otherwise, they must exchange worn pencils at the Supply Station as needed.

I tell the students they must have a pencil in order to obtain a pencil from the station.

Pencils

Pencil-Parting Party

Several times during the year, throw a pencil-parting party. All old, used, or abused pencils are placed in the exchange can in the Station, and each student gets a new pencil.

Friendly Reminders

Remember, you can try using peer pressure to keep pencils functional and clean. I do not allow students to verbally correct a classmate. Instead, as a class, they decide on a visual signal to be used as a reminder, such as pointing to their own pencil or tapping their pencil on the desk once. Students who do not stop chewing their pencils might be asked to keep the pencils they have defaced, and use them until they feel they can join the rest of the class in the pencil exchange. Place the responsibility for this decision on the student. Tell them to come to you when they feel they are ready to care for the pencils so they can be used by everyone.

Pencil Collection

Ask students to bring lost-and-found pencils to class to add to the collection. Students become scavengers, collecting lost pencils for your pencil supply. Continue to collect pencils from businesses that use them for advertising. These extra pencils are great for students who attend special classes where they must supply their own pencils. Remember, if at all possible, do not allow Supply Station pencils to leave your room.

Is pencil lead poisonous? Today it is nearly impossible to find pencils made with lead. Manufacturers have used graphite for years. However, as with any wound, a pencil puncture should be treated by your school nurse.

Pencils

Making A Pen Or Pencil "Pen"
It is difficult to monitor students and determine if they have pencils before going to or returning from other classrooms. And it is frustrating and time consuming to find pencils for students who arrive for class without a pencil.

Try this technique for students who attend special classes, or for departmentalized situations.

Make a simple pencil holder to keep by the door. Drill a series of ¼" holes in a 12"-long 2x4 or 2x6 wood board. Use your initials, a shape, or the number of your classroom for the pattern of holes.

Upon entering the classroom, students take their pencils and proceed to their work area. (This can also serve as a quick roll check.) As students leave and pencils are replaced you can see immediately if pencils are being taken from the room.

Note From Dinah
Throughout this book I stress the importance of having a place or space for everything so everything can be returned to its place. This not only organizes a classroom visually, but it seriously cuts "theft" and the misplacement of objects. I have found that pencils in a box will disappear much faster than pencils placed in individual spaces. A pencil missing from a pile of other pencils is not noticed, but an empty space in a pencil holder is definitely noticed.

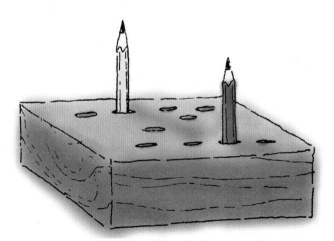

Ink Pens

Pen Pointers

With a few variations, use the same basic rules for pens as for pencils. If pens are used frequently, keep extras in the Supply Center; otherwise, keep them in your desk and allow a student to bring a faulty pen to you for exchange. Again, banks, insurance companies, or anyone using pens as a form of advertisement are sometimes willing to donate enough pens to supply your class with extras. Students should not bring pens that have special value.

Pencil/Pen Holder Using Dinah's Sentence Strip Holder Fold*

A Sentence Strip Holder can be used to hold pencils and pens (Photo, right). See photos below to make one.

You can label the pencil/pen holder (above) with the student's name, subject, or workstation name.

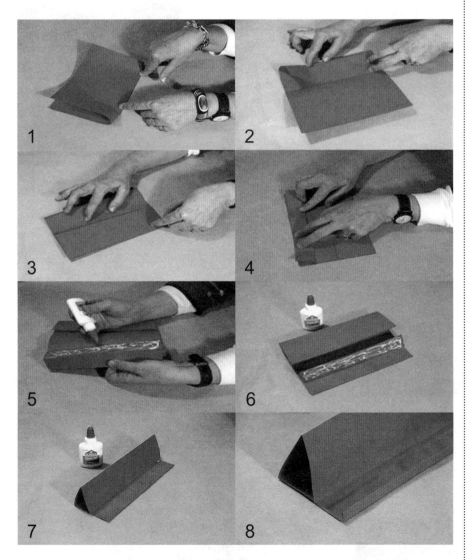

*From Dinah Zike's **Big Book of Books and Activities** and other Dinah Zike publications.

Small glue containers are much easier for students to use and for teachers to store. Glue sticks work well for some teachers and students, but I always prefered liquid glue.

Glue

"Just a Dot! Just a Dot!"

A national researcher concluded that as much as 60% of all mustard sold is wasted through overuse. Imagine what that figure would be if researchers focused on wasted glue!

For some reason, students of all ages have difficulty understanding the phrases "use only a dot!" or "just a dot" as I used to say. Use these tips to facilitate comprehension.

Get The Glue Flowing

On your school supply list, ask students to bring a small (1.2-ounce) bottle of glue and a large bottle of glue (12-ounce or larger) for refilling the small bottle.

If your supply list is already determined and you have funding available, you might order the 1.2-ounce bottles by the dozen from local office supply stores, and a gallon of glue for refills. Check internet prices, too. When using a gallon of glue for refills, fill an empty dishwashing liquid container (right). Students can use this to refill their own small containers.

Small, 1.2-ounce containers last longer than larger containers because they discourage overuse, take up less desk space, and are easier for small hands to handle. Plus, I have always found the following to be true: if kids have "a lot" they use a lot, if they have only "a little" they use less.

Petroleum Jelly to the Rescue!

Note From Dinah

During my first years as a teacher, I asked students to bring the largest glue containers available on the market to use at their desks with hopes that they would last the entire school year. Within the first week, students mutilated the glue caps with their scissors or other sharp objects trying to open the dried, clogged tips. Then I would see them use both hands to hold and squeeze the heavy glue containers. As they were squeezing too hard and trying to hold the glue containers, a force called "gravity" was pulling the glue down and out in torrents. I was walking around the room, vainly repeating over and over, "Just a dot! Just a dot!"

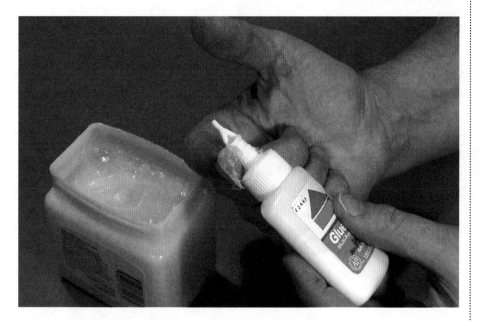

I solved the problem of dried and/or clogged glue bottle tips by pulling off the glue cap, coating the threads of the screw with petroleum jelly, and replacing the cap. It now opens and closes easily, and students do not have to dig out the dried glue in the cap. When using petroleum jelly on the caps of small glue containers, students are able to place "just a dot" without difficulty.

Glue

Projects Using Glue

For projects requiring frequent use of small amounts of glue, squirt glue into a small jar lid or a container such as those used for tea-light candles. Hot glue this container onto the middle of a plastic margarine dish or coffee can lid. Students use cotton swabs to disperse the glue. When not in use, the cotton swab rests on the lid.

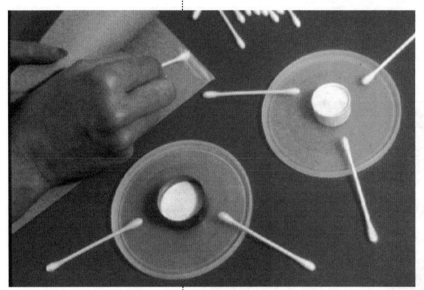

Other Glue Tips

Small plastic bottles with pointed caps make excellent glue containers. Check to see if a local beauty salon or beauty supply house will sell (or donate) several for your class. Puncture small holes in the spouts to prevent overuse.

Glue Art

Trace along the lines of a coloring sheet with liquid glue. Allow glue to dry thoroughly. Place a clean sheet of paper over the dried, raised outline. Rub a crayon or chalk over the paper and watch the drawing appear as if by magic.

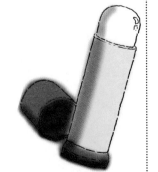

Note From Dinah

I do not like glue sticks. They dry out, break off, and do not "wet" the papers to be glued enough to prevent them from separating later. Glue sticks are often necessary for students with gross motor skill difficulties, but with practice, most students can learn to use liquid glue. Do not forget the petroleum jelly. (See page 15.)

Glue

Lock 'Er Up

When possible, give students the responsibility of maintaining their own supplies. However, as you know, many cannot resist the temptation to play with their glue. I have had students use glue to make false fingernails, molded sculptures, and unsolicited art projects which all result in wasted glue.

Use small boxes, such as Velveeta® cheese boxes, to create your Lock 'Er Up lockers. You can brighten them with paint if you have time.

Your Lock 'Er Up area should be used to head off wastefulness. It works well with other school supplies, too (e.g., carelessness with scissors, markers, etc.). This locker can be made to look like student lockers by placing cheese boxes together as shown.

Make it undesirable not to be able to keep one's own supplies. Have a sign-in and sign-out sheet at the lockers for students who have had their supplies taken from them as a consequence. They must now check them in and out with each use. (This can also be used to reinforce writing time to the minute. Example: Out: 12:13, In: 12:22)

After the first offense, allow students to apologize for the misuse of their supplies, and to state they will be more responsible in the future. On second and third offenses, the supplies must be kept in the locker. It is the student's responsibility to inform the teacher when he/she feels ready to take responsibility for properly using their supplies.

Glue

Colorful Glue

You can make beautiful, pastel colored glue (photo, left) for your classroom art area or tactile learning centers by adding a few drops of food coloring to glue containers, then shaking the glue bottle vigorously until the color is evenly distributed. Cake icing dye can also be used to make glues of unusual colors. Using a toothpick, place a small piece of the paste dye into the bottle of white glue. Shake vigorously until the color is blended throughout.

Rubber Cement: Teacher Use Only

Rubber cement should be used in well ventilated areas. Teachers find it advantageous over water-based glues for bulletin boards and teacher-created instructional aids since it does not bind permanently and does not leave glue lines that show through the glued object.

Spray Adhesive: Teacher Use Only

Spray adhesives have the mounting properties of rubber cement in a spray container. Objects can be glued evenly without spots showing through or edges peeling upward. Spray adhesives must be stored securely and kept from children and used in well-ventilated work rooms or better yet, outside. Be careful with the overspray.

Teacher's Responsibility: Hazardous Materials

It is your responsibility to familiarize yourself with your district's guidelines and policies regarding the use and storage of hazardous materials.

THREE DIMENSIONAL GLUE
Colored glue makes two-dimensional illustrations look and feel tactile. The following examples illustrate ways to use colored glue:
A. Make topographical maps by adding layers of glue to maps. (Allow each layer to dry before adding the next layer.)
B. Color the percentages, locations on maps, or important parts of diagrams and illustrations.
C. Color fractional parts.
D. Make letters, numbers, or shapes tactile by adding dots of glue to infill areas.

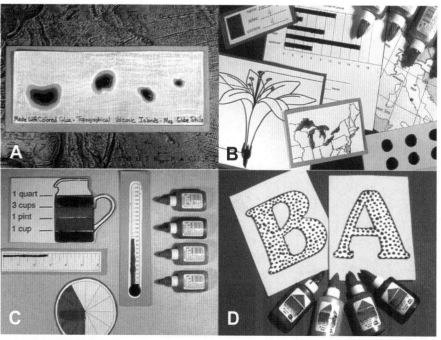

Glue Recipes

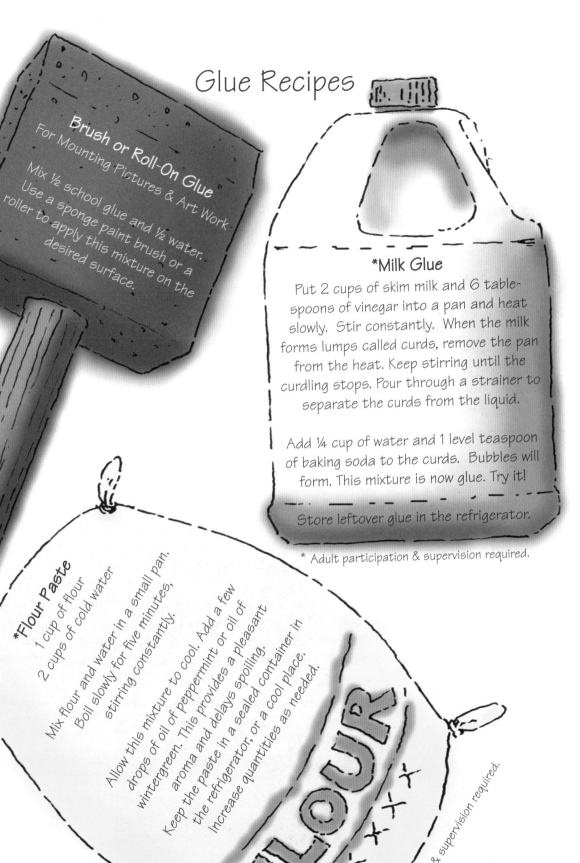

Brush or Roll-On Glue
For Mounting Pictures & Art Work

Mix ½ school glue and ½ water. Use a sponge paint brush or a roller to apply this mixture on the desired surface.

*Milk Glue

Put 2 cups of skim milk and 6 tablespoons of vinegar into a pan and heat slowly. Stir constantly. When the milk forms lumps called curds, remove the pan from the heat. Keep stirring until the curdling stops. Pour through a strainer to separate the curds from the liquid.

Add ¼ cup of water and 1 level teaspoon of baking soda to the curds. Bubbles will form. This mixture is now glue. Try it!

Store leftover glue in the refrigerator.

* Adult participation & supervision required.

*Flour Paste
1 cup of flour
2 cups of cold water

Mix flour and water in a small pan. Boil slowly for five minutes, stirring constantly.

Allow this mixture to cool. Add a few drops of oil of peppermint or oil of wintergreen. This provides a pleasant aroma and delays spoiling. Keep the paste in a sealed container in the refrigerator, or a cool place. Increase quantities as needed.

* Adult participation & supervision required.

Scissors

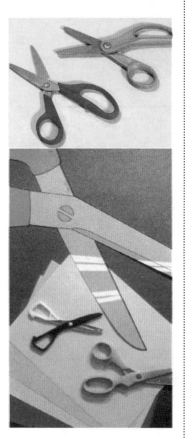

DON'T CUT CORNERS
On your yearly school supply list, ask parents to furnish good scissors appropriate to your grade level.

My favorite scissors are 5½" in length and have pointed tips. I use a long, leather cord around my neck to keep them handy and store them in a pocket when not in use. I recommend teachers use blunt-ended scissors when working with young children.

Cut Ups!

Students are natural "cut-ups." Allow time and provide opportunities for development of the fine motor skill of cutting. Cutting is an excellent eye/hand coordination activity and a practical life skill. Practice will ensure that future cutting projects are accomplished quickly.

Try these cutting activities using scratch paper, paper scraps, or discarded paper found near a photocopy machine or printer:

- Cut paper in half. (See page 21).
- Follow lines, trying to cut without the line showing on either side of the cut.
- Cut slits in the center of paper.
- Cut designs or shapes in the center of paper.
- Cut symmetrical patterns out of folded paper, etc.

Cut It Out!

Treat students' scissors the same as glue. Use the Lock 'Er Up area for students who misuse their scissors.

Note From Dinah

It is my trademark to wear scissors around my neck as a "necklace." As you might imagine, this habit of nearly 35 years began because I could never find my scissors when I needed them. I usually wear jackets or smocks with pockets, and I slip my scissors into a pocket when they are not in use. This keeps them from being a danger to others as I bend over children working at tables, and as I move between rows of desks.

Scissors

Shaving With Scissors: How To Cut Along A Fold

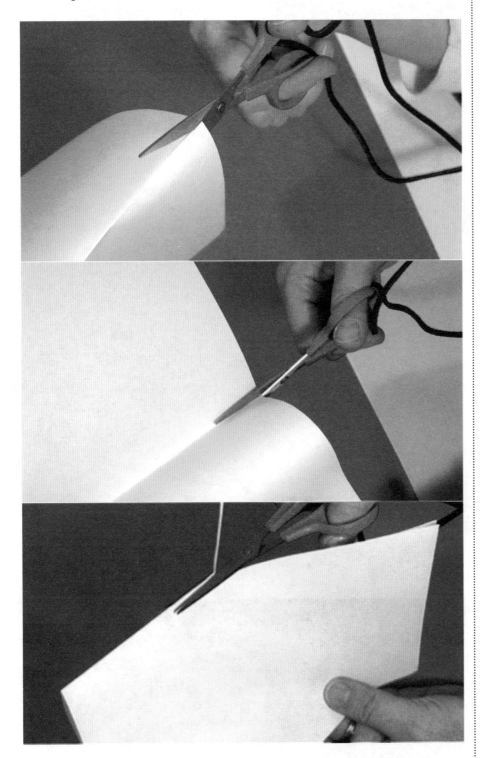

It is difficult to cut along a paper fold. If students cut along the "mountain" of the fold, it is nearly impossible to cut accurately along the fold line.

If students cut along the "valley" of the fold, the sides of the paper obstruct the student's view of the fold, making it difficult to cut.

The fastest method for cutting folded paper is to shave off the paper fold itself! This makes cutting easier for all ages.

Crayons

New Crayons

For younger students there is probably no other school supply quite like their brand-new crayons; but have you noticed that students take care of their crayons for about as long as the new crayon box stays intact? When the box is gone, the crayons are borrowed, broken, and lost.

Can Crayons Create Chaos?

Debbie calls you over to her desk. Near tears, she explains, "Daniel has my green and he won't give it back?" Danny sits there, shaking his head, declaring that the green crayon is his. What do you do? Break the crayon and give half to each? Play detective and try to solve the problem through logic? Either way might be acceptable, but a little philosophy is even better, "Neither a borrower nor a lender be."

CLASSROOM RULE:
NO STUDENT CAN BORROW A CRAYON FROM ANOTHER STUDENT.
NO STUDENT CAN LEND A CRAYON TO ANOTHER STUDENT.

Use crayon cans in the classroom supply station and/or publishing center. Note how the shelf has been covered with bulletin board paper, and blue circles have been glued onto the paper to indicate where the cans are to be placed. This will help keep your publishing center organized.

Crayons

Crayon Supply Station

With the crayon rule in mind, obtain several small vegetable cans or coffee cans for your Supply Station. Cover them with white, colored, or contact paper. Each can holds extra crayons of one color and its varying shades. For example, one container might hold dark green, lime green, and other shades of green. Decorate the can covers if desired.

When students are missing a particular color of crayon, they go to the Supply Station and get the crayon they need. This crayon becomes their property, and they do not return it to the crayon can.

When a student finds a crayon on the floor, there is no discussion as to who owns it. The student places it into the appropriate crayon can. This also encourages students to retrieve lost/found crayons on campus and to bring their old crayons from home. They love sorting their old crayons into the cans in the Supply Station.

Student Helpers keep crayons sorted and organized in the Supply Station.

Giant Crayons

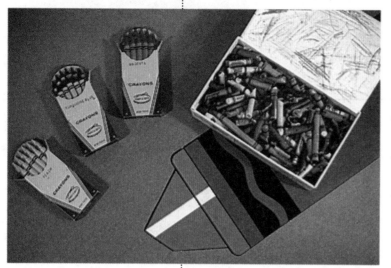

Bring Me Your Broken And Paperless!

Used crayons are needed to fill your Supply Station cans and to make giant crayons. Collect them from year to year. Have students bring old crayons from home. You can even ask for them on your Supply List. Students who bring used crayons from home are allowed to sort them into the crayon cans.

Giant Crayons For Giant Creations

Students love giant crayons. Giant crayons can be purchased, but it is simple to make your own. Giant crayons are perfect for the following: making rubbings of textured items, coloring large murals and bulletin boards, and creating colorful backdrops for plays, puppet shows, and other classroom productions.

Method #1:

Ask parents or grandparents to help with the following:
- Collect crayons and sort them by color.
- Remove all paper wrappers from crayons.
- Spray a muffin tin, coffee cups, or other ovenproof container with a spray cooking oil.
- To make solid color crayons, fill the container with crayon pieces of the same color.

Break crayons into 1/2" pieces. They do not need to be grated or crushed.

Giant Crayons

Method #1 Continued:

- Place the containers of broken crayons in a warm oven (right) at about 200 degrees.
- Allow crayons to melt slowly. Do not stir.
- When crayons are melted and all air space is gone, allow them to cool thoroughly – preferably overnight.
- Caution: Be patient, as crayons may be cool on the outside, but still hot and liquid inside.
- After 24 hours, when completely cool, remove the crayons from the containers.
- To make mixed-color crayons, fill the container with two or three different colors. Some useful color combinations are:

Brown, black and white = Land
Blues and white = Sky
Blues and greens = Water
Different shades of green = Trees, fields
Red, yellow, orange = Fire, lava, sun
Brown, white, beige = Sand, desert, beach

Large muffin tins (left) make big, thick crayons that last a long time and are perfect for coloring large areas of space. To the delight of the students, I recently used small muffin tins to make crayons that could be used at classroom tables and desks. I always say, "Kids love things that are larger than normal and smaller than usual."

Giant Crayons

Method #2:
Slowly melt crayons in tin cans in a warm oven (low temperature setting) or in a double boiler. To make easy-to-hold crayons, carefully pour the melted wax into small plastic drinking cups.

To make mixed color crayons using this method, fill each plastic cup with one color of crayon broken into small pieces. Pour melted crayons of a different color over the broken pieces.

Craft shops sell candy or lollipop molds in many shapes and sizes. Use one of them to make a "Crayon on a Rope." Cut a piece of string 3 feet long, and place the two ends into the liquid crayon. When it dries, you have a "Crayon on a Rope!"

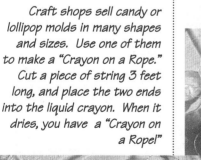

Shaped Crayons
Pour melted wax into candy molds to make shaped crayons. Use these special crayons in learning centers, or give them to students as rewards or holiday presents.

Watercolor Washes

Washing With Watercolors

Teachers and students can learn the simple technique of using water color washes to create projects, learning center activities, folder games, bulletin boards, flash cards, and other instructional aids.

Students young and old enjoy the involvement and hands-on experience of watercolors, which are less time consuming and less costly than felt tip markers.

For This Technique You Need:
- Watercolor cakes.
- Brushes of different sizes.
- Cans of fresh water.
- Paper towels for absorbing excess water and paint.
- Objects or projects to be painted.

Directions:
- Wet brush. Tap brush gently on edge of can to remove excess water, but allow some water to remain in the brush.
- Gently move the wet brush over one corner of the cake paint, allowing it to absorb the color.
- Move the brush across the area to be colored.
- Thoroughly clean brush before using another color.

Use this fast and inexpensive technique to add color to the following before laminating:
- Large bulletin board pictures and items made using an opaque projector.
- Learning Center activities that are black-line copy.
- Coloring book pictures used as identification activities, storytelling aids, sequencing cards, etc.
- Workbook pictures used on flash cards.
- Giant *Foldables*™ like a layered-look bulletin board (right).

Paints

Use brightly colored latex enamel* to paint classroom furniture, cardboard items, toys, etc.

*Teacher Use Only

Sponge brushes are fun and practical to use. Shapes cut out of kitchen sponges make great stencils.

To make water-based paint* thicker and smoother, add a mixture of paste made from corn-starch and water. To make paste, mix ¼ cup of corn-starch with one cup of cold water. Cook over a low heat until thick. Stir constantly.

*Adult spervision required

Chalkboard paint* is avail-able in slate black or chalk-board green. It is usually oil based, so use brushes that can be discard-ed or have paint cleaner* available.

*Teacher Use Only

Small condiment containers from fast-food restaurants make handy individual paint containers for desks or learning stations.

If students spill water-based paint in the classroom, sprinkle baking soda on the paint to absorb it before cleaning.

Paint Recipes

Paint Recipes

These paint recipes are easy and inexpensive to make, and the results are fun to use.

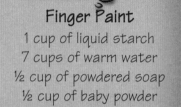

Finger Paint

1 cup of liquid starch
7 cups of warm water
½ cup of powdered soap
½ cup of baby powder

Slowly pour and stir the soap into the water and allow it to stand for 15 minutes. Mix the baby powder into the starch, and add it to the soap and water. Mix well. Add food coloring or powdered tempera paint.

*Cornstarch Paint

½ cup of cornstarch
1 package gelatin

Mix package of gelatin in ¼ cup of water in a bowl. Boil ¾ cup water in a small pan and mix in the cornstarch. Add 2 cups of water and bring to boil. Reduce to medium heat until the liquid is clear. Quickly add gelatin and remove from the burner. Add powdered tempera paint for color.

Quick Starch Paint

2 cups of powdered soap
½ cup of liquid starch

Mix together with an electric mixer. Add food coloring or powdered tempera paint.

* Adult participation & supervision required

Markers & Colored Pencils

Note from Dinah

I prefer to use supplies that "multiply and divide." For example, crayons "multiply and divide" as they are broken and as students contribute used ones to the class supply. Markers and colored pencils do not "multiply and divide" on their own, so I devised a method of using only a few at a time in order to always have replacements. I prefer that students use colored pencils for *Foldables*™ instead of markers since they do not bleed through the paper.

Students love markers. They love to "tattoo" themselves with the bright colors. They love to take the center filters out and place them in glue bottles to make colored glue. And, they love to paint their fingernails.

A Few At A Time

Since it is more difficult to replace markers and colored pencils than crayons, it might be preferable to store them away in a closet. Collect them at the end of the first week of school. On the first day of school explain that markers will be collected at that time. That allows students to have time to enjoy their new supplies before they go into storage.

Make four to six containers of markers or colored pencils to be shared by groups of students. Place two of each color in each container. They can be replaced using the surplus markers and colored pencils stored in your closet.

Overhead Projector Markers

Overhead Projector Markers
Use overhead projector markers for writing on acetate-covered work-sheets, vinyl-covered bulletin boards, and work tables. (Also see the section on bulletin boards, page 107.)

Note From Dinah
Using wet paper towels to swipe off water-based markers creates liquid dye that quickly dirties hands, desks, and papers.

I must confess, when stranded at the overhead projector without a wet paper towel or access to water, I have been known to wet a dry towel with saliva to wipe off the writing from a transparency. This very efficient but unsanitary method of removing marker—a little bit of wet with a whole lot of dry—works great, but there is a better way. The same result can be achieved using the technique below.

Computers are commonly used to present information to students, but many teachers say they still need and use their overhead projectors.

Cleaning Water-Based Markers
1. Use a small container that can be sealed, such as a small butter tub, soap dish, or resealable plastic bag.
2. Fold several paper towels to fit in the container (photo A).
3. Mix equal parts of rubbing alcohol and water. Pour over paper towels until they are saturated and there is a small surplus of liquid in the container.
4. Slightly dampen a dry paper towel by touching it to the wet towels (photo A). Use this mostly dry towel to remove marker writing (photo B). Refresh the wet towels by spraying them with the alcohol and water mixture as needed.

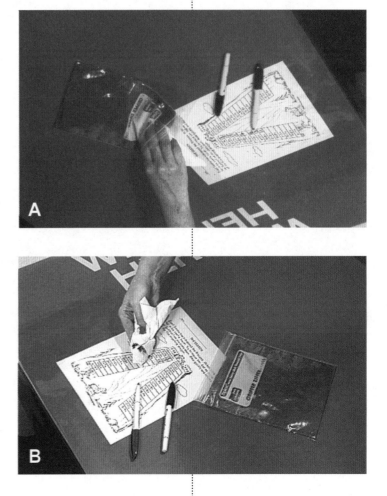

Overhead Projector Markers

Practice Makes Perfect

1. Place practice worksheets in acetate sleeves or large resealable plastic bags. Two worksheets (front and back) can be used per sleeve.
2. Paper clip or spring clip worksheets into the sleeves to keep them stable as students write and erase.
3. Use overhead projector markers or wipe-off markers to complete these sealed activity sheets.

Examples Of Practice Sheet Combinations:

- United States map/world map.
- United States map/state map.
- Continent map/country map.
- Spelling word list and an activity using the spelling words.
- Language arts skills practice activities, for example:
    - Circle all punctuation on a photocopied page.
    - Fill in missing punctuation.
    - Highlight parts of speech.
- Letter formation practice sheet and an activity where students write words containing the featured letters.

Note From Dinah

Wax pencils can be used on acetate sheets and on vinyl, but they are very difficult to erase. I frequently use dry-erase markers.

For Teachers Only

If you should use permanent markers on acetate, plastic, or vinyl, try using fingernail polish remover or hairspray to remove the marker. Remember these are toxic substances and should NOT be used by students. Check your school policy on use of hazardous materials.

Non-toxic Alternative

Artist's rubber erasers, purchased at an art supply store, can be used as a non-toxic alternative to remove permanent marker from a slick surface.

Write Here, On the Table

Clear Vinyl

Sheets of clear vinyl can be purchased in different thicknesses and weights. It is available in rolls at art supply and fabric stores. Like bolts of fabric, these may be purchased in any length.

1. Cover a table with bright bulletin board paper or seasonal wrapping paper. (The table pictured is a door placed on cinder block legs.)

2. Insert several different practice or drill worksheets under the vinyl around the outer edges of the table. Allow students to use overhead projector markers to complete the practice sheets by writing on the table. Students can return to the table to work on different activity sheets during "free time" or teacher-designated times.

3. Have a file folder with check sheets available, or place check sheets in acetate pockets.

4. Upon completion, students check and correct their work, possibly sharing it with a "witness" or partner.

5. Teach students to use the method outlined on page 31 to clean the work area and make it ready for others.

Storing Supplies

Keeping Up With Supplies

Students need to learn at an early age to take care of their personal possessions. School supplies are no exception. As often as possible, give students the responsibility of maintaining their own supplies either at their desks or in a special storage area.

Keep a Lid On

If your students use cardboard supply boxes for storing desk materials, place a two-inch strip of clear tape along the hinge line of the box. This will help keep it intact for the duration of the school year.

Can Do Storage

Use large coffee cans or cardboard chip canisters for storing supplies. Place the plastic lid on the bottom of the can to lower the noise level when in use. Glue paper around the cans, and label accordingly.

Stacked Storage

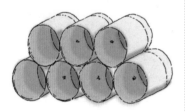

Five-gallon ice cream containers from ice cream shops stack nicely on their sides to provide storage for larger possessions. Punch small holes in the sides, and connect them with brass brads, or tie with yarn.

Use hot glue or Velcro® to attach stacked coffee cans together. Double-sided foam tape also works well.

Small, strong cardboard boxes from grocery stores can be painted and stacked uniformly for storage of lightweight objects.

Cereal Box Storage

Small Cereal Boxes

Use small cereal boxes to store audio tapes. Ask each student to bring a blank audio tape at the beginning of the year. Use the tapes to record individual student reading and oral reports.

Tape recordings are excellent assessment tools, and can be used to document student growth and progress. Students often forget how much they have learned. If they hear their progress, they feel smart! Use the tapes as a Mother's Day gift, or present them to parents at an end-of-the-year parent conference.

Large Cereal Boxes

Use large cereal boxes to store examples of student work, class work, and projects by units, themes, text chapters, or titles of literature. When review is needed, examine the contents of the appropriate box. For example, collect student papers and projects on insects in a cereal box during the first month of school. When a student brings a butterfly for students to investigate four months later, review what students remember about insects and examine the contents of the insect box to reinforce previously learned concepts and information.

Trash

Trash Cans

Where do you place the trash cans in your classroom? According to a recent survey, most teachers place the classroom trash can next to their desk. Moving it will eliminate some of those unnecessary student trips to the wastebasket.

Tricks With Trash

Replace the large trash can by your desk with a small rectangular one that fits beneath your desk. This trash can is for your use only. This helps keep your thrown-away notes and papers confidential, and if you toss something by accident it is easily retrieved. For an easy, inexpensive trash can, cut off the top of a giant-sized detergent box, and paint or cover with contact paper (photo below). Grocery sacks may be used to line these small trash boxes.

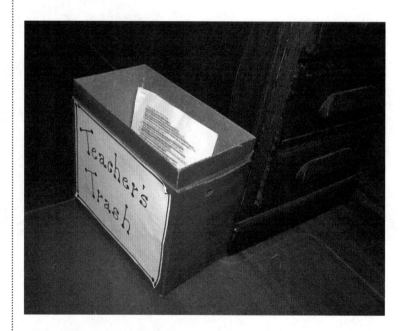

Have several larger trash cans in the room for student use: one by the door, and another at a heavily-traveled area of the room.

Your Trash Can Helper Performs The Following Tasks:
- Empties your personal trash into the larger classroom cans at the end of the day.
- Places all trash cans by the door at the end of the day for easy emptying by the custodian.
- Upon arriving in the morning, puts all trash cans back in their permanent positions.

Trash

Making Mountains Out Of Mole Hills

Five hundred sheets of paper is about a two-inch stack. Five hundred sheets of wadded paper will fill at least three large classroom trashcans. Teach students to <u>fold</u> their trash (lower right corner to upper left corner, or another unusual fold) to take up less space on their desks and in the trashcan. Folding also prevents unnecessary noise and action. Notice that television newscasters will often fold the sheet of paper from which they have just read, preventing the next news story from getting mixed up with the previous story.

Pass The Trash!

Have a trash container for each row of desks in the room. One-gallon plastic milk jugs cut so that the handle is still intact (right) make excellent containers that are easy to pass around. At several intervals during the day, or during cutting activities, say, "Pass the trash!" The container is passed down the row. Your Trash Can Helper is responsible for distributing and emptying them.

Table Top Trashcan

Place a small trash container on each table and let your Helper monitor these as well.

Paper Wads

Most students love wadding up paper and making trips to the trash can. They don't seem to realize that trash paper can actually sit on their desk for long periods of time without causing harm to the desk or themselves! Have students keep their trash until a class break or until they pass a trash can.

Photographs for Identity

Classroom Photographs

Method 1, Film Camera: Photograph students in groups of three or four. Get as close as possible. Print the photos, and cut out close-ups of each student's head. Tape these "head shots" to a single 8½" x 11" sheet of paper. Make twenty or more photocopies of the page. Use a paper cutter to cut the photographs apart. Place copies of each student's photograph inside individual envelopes as pictured.

1. Take group pictures.
2. Cut out each head and place as many "head shots" as possible on one sheet of paper.
3. Use small "change" envelopes (2 1/4" x 3 1/2") to make storage pockets for student photos. To make pockets, seal each envelope, and cut off the fold along one of the long sides.
4. Glue a student photo to the front of each, and glue the envelope pockets to a piece of poster board.

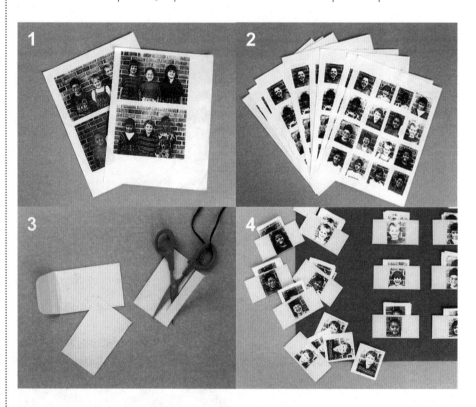

Method 2, Digital Camera: Photograph students. Use a computer to crop and place the "head shots" onto one 8½ x 11 sheet of paper. Print as many copies as desired, or print a master copy and use it to make photocopies. Cut photos apart and place in envelopes for easy student access.

Photo Organization And Storage

Glue the envelopes onto a poster board and fill each envelope with multiple copies of each student's photo (left). This board organizes and stores the photos for easy access. The photos are used on projects, journals, reports, and more.

Classroom Jobs

Have Students Do The Work

Dozens of daily tasks must be completed for your classroom to operate smoothly and at top efficiency. However, it is not mandatory, necessary, or even preferable that all of those tasks be performed by you, the teacher.

Note From Dinah

When I began teaching, I had a helper's chart that I purchased at a teacher supply store. It was beautiful, and I dutifully wrote each student's name on a card, placed the cards in the chart pockets, and vowed to myself that I would move them the first thing every Monday morning, thus changing the helpers. I was good at this for about a month, and then I forgot to move the name cards. A couple of hours into the day, a student exclaimed, "Mrs. Zike, you forgot to change the helpers!" I apologized, ask them to do their jobs from last week, and promised that I would change the chart as soon as I completed my current task. Two days later, when students complained that I still had not changed the helpers, I loudly proclaimed that since the week was nearly over students should continue old jobs until the next Monday. I hate to admit it, but there were times when several weeks would pass in this fashion. Students did not take their jobs seriously because they saw that I did not take their jobs seriously. This only resulted in more work for me, so I wrote this down on an index card as a problem. A practical solution is on the next page.

Make a "Helping Hand" folder. Place important papers or notices to be taken home at the end of the day in the folder, and have a student helper hand out the papers before students leave the classroom. Student helpers enjoy this responsibility, and it prevents teachers from running down halls and getting onto buses searching for students who were not given notices or other handouts before the end of the school day.

Classroom Jobs & Helper's Wheel

Lots Of Jobs

Make a list of every task that students could do to help you. Assign as many classroom jobs to students as possible, and use these daily activities to teach responsibility. No matter what the student's academic level, they will find that nothing is more rewarding than a job well done. When each student is assigned a task that takes only a few minutes each day, you have saved yourself a lot of unnecessary work, and freed an hour or more of your precious planning and instructional time!

Note From Dinah

Over thirty years ago I designed a simple Helper's Wheel that makes it easy to designate Helpers for the day or week. With only a small turn of the inner wheel the Helpers change tasks in a matter of seconds rather than valuable minutes.

Teacher's Tip

Change jobs weekly instead of daily. This allows for mastery of the task and results in less confusion.

Helper's Wheel

Wheel Pattern

Use the corresponding wheel pattern to make your Helper's Job Wheel (see page 55), or make your own pattern.

Self-Contained Classrooms

Place one or two names in each section. In sections where only one student's name is used, select students who are seldom absent.

When placing two names in a section, pair students who remain in the classroom with students who frequently leave the room for special classes. Or place a student who is never absent with a student who has numerous absences. This assures someone will usually be present to help with the assigned job.

Departmentalized Classrooms

In departmentalized situations, use numbers in the grade book instead of names on the Helper's Wheel. For non-readers, use symbols (colored shapes, pictures of animals, etc.) to represent individual students.

Transient Students

If you have transient students in your class, use a Helper's Wheel that has numbers instead of student names on the outer wheel. The numbers correspond to the student numbers in your grade book. If a student moves away, a job is left vacant. When a new student is added in the vacated grade book slot, this job is filled. At the beginning of the year the grade book is organized alphabetically, but it will gradually become numeric as the year progresses and students come and go. See page 72.

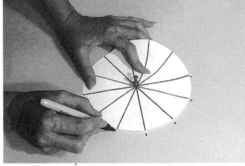

Place a push pin through the center of the pattern, and mark the sections on a sheet of posterboard or cardboard.

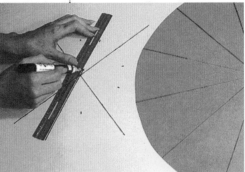

Connect the marks making sure the lines pass through the center hole made by the push pin. Make two posterboard circles, one smaller than the other, using the same pattern.

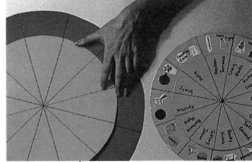

Place the smaller circle inside the larger one and connect them with a brad.

Job Descriptions & Training

On-The-Job Training (Very Important!)
Spend the first few weeks of school teaching the entire class how to perform the classroom jobs before using the Helper's Wheel. Demonstrate the appropriate way to complete a task. Then ask a student to perform the task you demonstrated as the class watches. This is very important. If you skip this step, you will be re-teaching every job each week as students rotate into new jobs.

Sample Jobs
Helping Hand: Passes out papers and supplies, and helps distribute papers that are sent home (PTA announcements, book club news, etc.) See page 39 for Helping Hand ideas.

Trash Can Helper: Empties and/or monitors all trash cans and containers in the room(see pages 36,37).

Class Leader: First in line each time students line up. (Now students race to be second or last, instead of first!) See "Lining Up" for more information(see page 84).

Drill Sergeant: Leads the pledge to the flag and other class recitations (see page 45).

Electrician/Technology Expert: Turns the lights on or off upon entering or leaving the classroom, and helps the teacher with any other technology (computers, overhead slide projects, etc.)

Zoologist/Animal Keeper: If you are allowed to keep live animals in your classroom, this Helper cares for classroom pets on a daily basis. Know your district's policy on animals in the classroom.

Paper Helper: Places all papers to be graded in numerical order, and helps the teacher distribute and collect student work. (See section on grade book, page 71.)

Photocopy the icons above and those on the opposite page. Cut out each one, and place them on the Helper's Wheel.

Job Descriptions

Sample Jobs

Cafeteria Helper: Helps with trays, trash removal, noise control, and reports to the teacher any problems that arise during lunch.

Pencil Helper: Sharpens all pencils at a designated time, or supervises the sharpening of pencils to prevent waste. (see page 10)

Desk Helper: Keeps desks or tables clean and in line. Checks that chairs are pushed under or placed on top of desks at the end of the day.

Board Helper: Chalkboard, Eraserboard, and/or Bulletin Boards
Keeps erasers and markers clean, and cleans boards when instructed to do so. Helps teacher assemble and disassemble bulletin boards, and helps keep bulletin boards clean and organized.

Botanist/Gardener: Takes care of classroom plants by giving each plant one tablespoon or coffee scoop full of water each day. This prevents overwatering and root rot while providing daily care. Know your district's policy on plants in the classroom.

Game Show Host: Leads the class or groups of students in classroom games, such as Map and Globe, Family Feud, Concentration, Password, and others.

Sink Helper: Keeps the sink and surrounding area clean and neat without using chemicals for cleaning.

Job Descriptions

Sample Jobs

Academic Helpers: Recruit as many of these as you need. These Helpers hand out items relevant to the subject of study, and are also in charge of Learning Center materials based on that subject.

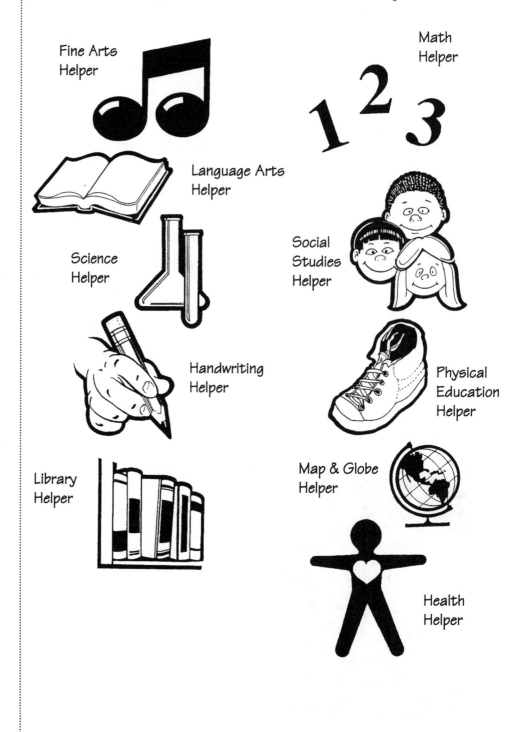

Fine Arts
Helper

Math
Helper

Language Arts
Helper

Science
Helper

Social
Studies
Helper

Handwriting
Helper

Physical
Education
Helper

Library
Helper

Map & Globe
Helper

Health
Helper

Pledge to the Flag

Note From Dinah

One year my students wanted to sit when they should be standing, and stand when they should be sitting. While standing to say the pledge, they leaned on their desks, shifted feet, and several stayed poised to race to their chairs before anyone was seated. This was a problem that began to irritate me. I wanted all students to stand and respectfully say the pledge. I wrote the problem on an index card, and it lay hidden on my desk under stacks of paper for weeks.

Lou Gossett Jr. Came To My Rescue

One day, shortly after seeing Lou Gossett Jr. as a drill sergeant in the movie *An Officer and a Gentleman*, I was sitting in church remembering the procedure my minister used for saying the Pledge at a summer Bible School session. This gave me an inspirational idea! By combining Lou Gossett Jr. and my minister, the pledge problem was solved! The "Drill Sergeant" position was created and added to my helper's wheel.

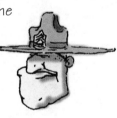

Teach The Class The Following Procedure:

Drill Sergeant: "Attention!"
Students stand erect and place hands at side.
Drill Sergeant: "Salute!"
Students place hands over hearts.
Drill Sergeant: "Pledge!"
Students: "I pledge allegiance….."

This procedure also works well with state flag pledges.

Pledge to the Flag

Rally Round The Flag

Schedule times for your class to raise the flag on the school grounds during the year. If appropriate, after raising the flag, have your students say national and/or state pledges and sing patriotic songs.

Remember, the flag should be "hoisted briskly and lowered ceremoniously." A flag does not have to be destroyed if it touches the ground, but great caution should be used to prevent this from happening.

Note: You may have students whose parents do not wish them to participate in these activities. Have these students do something special for you during this time. It is better for them to be active than to be sitting and waiting for others to finish something in which they cannot participate.

Folding The Flag

Teach your class these steps for properly folding the U.S. flag:

1.

2.

3.

4.

5.

Tuck in the flap

6.

Handwriting Tablets & Notebook Paper

Do It Yourself

As with many supplies some students invariably bring the wrong materials, even when exact specifications for handwriting tablets or writing paper are given. If at all possible, relieve parents and students of this responsibility.

Teacher Tip

Investigate your district's policies regarding the collection of money from students before using this procedure.

Have students bring the least amount of money possible that will allow you to purchase handwriting paper or notebook paper in bulk for the classroom. Dollar discount stores often have large supplies of inexpensive paper, and for one or two dollars per child parents can be guaranteed that they will not have to buy more paper during the school year. Buy and/or collect packets of paper, and stack them in a corner until needed. I tie them with cord to prevent reams from "disappearing."

Order In Bulk

Grade-specific handwriting paper can be ordered by the ream or the case from teacher supply stores and paper companies, usually at substantial savings over retail handwriting tablet prices.

Advantages Of This Procedure:

• All paper is exactly alike.
• It is not attached to a binder that causes tearing.
• It can be stored in an open basket in the Handwriting Center or Supply Station.
• It is not in the students' possession, and thus is not wasted.

Buy and/or collect packets of paper and stack them in a corner until needed. I tie them with cord or store them away to prevent reams from "disappearing."

Publishing Center
Solving Paper Problems

I have a small paper cutter locked away in a supply cabinet for my personal use. NEVER allow sutdents to use a paper cutter.

Note From Dinah

When I was teaching and I asked students to "take out a sheet of paper" for a writing activity, not every student had paper. They either never brought any, used up what they had and forgot to tell their parents they needed more, or they wasted away their last sheet minutes before they needed it for the day's graded activity. So what did they do? They borrowed paper from their neighbors or from students on the other side of the room.

Once all students had a sheet of paper, the questions began. "How many lines?" was usually first. Then, "Is this for a grade?." Depending on the class and the writing activity, I heard questions such as, "Does it have to be in cursive?", "Do I have to use a pen?", "Does spelling count?"

One particularly difficult year, after having been asked over and over again, "How many lines?" and repeatedly answering in various creative ways, I snapped. I picked up a new ream of 500 sheets of notebook paper, marched to the teachers' workroom while ripping off the plastic covering the paper. I placed all 500 sheets under a guillotine-sized paper cutter, and tried to cut all 500 sheets in half at once! And after several attempts, believe me, I was successful!

I marched myself back into the classroom, waved the 1,000 half-sheets of paper at the class, and said, **"This is how many lines! Don't ask me how many lines! This is how many lines!"** Little did I know at the time that my frustration and drastic actions would result in the beginning of my Publishing Center, which is currently used by teachers internationally (see pages 49-61)

Publishing Center
Writing a Little, a Lot

Smaller Sheets

There is something about using a half sheet of paper that entirely changes students' attitudes toward writing. When students are given a whole sheet of paper and ask to write half a page, it seems more imposing, and it often takes them four times as long to finish as if instead they had been given half a sheet of paper for the same assignment.

Psychologically, a half-sheet or a quarter-sheet of paper seems to imply, "This is easy. It can be finished quickly." (See quarter-sheet patterns, page 51.)

Picture Frames

Use small picture frames to illustrate and feature a person, place, or thing. (See pattern p. 51.)

Notice the quarter- and half-sheet sized paper displayed and ready for student use in this publishing center. For other storage and organization ideas see pages 128 - 132..

Publishing Center
Quarter-Sheets & Picture Frames

Useful Tools

Use small picture frames to illustrate and feature a person, place, or thing.

Use quarter-sheets or half-sheets of notebook paper and small picture frames to integrate the following:
-Narrative, descriptive, expository, and persuasive writing.
-Main ideas and supporting facts.
-Self questioning .
-Terms and definitions.
-Important people, places, things & more!

Publishing Center
Quarter-Sheet & Picture Frame Reproducibles

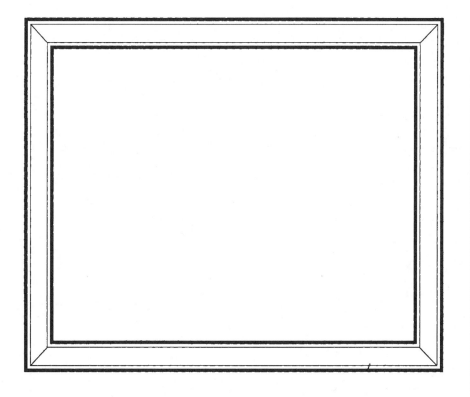

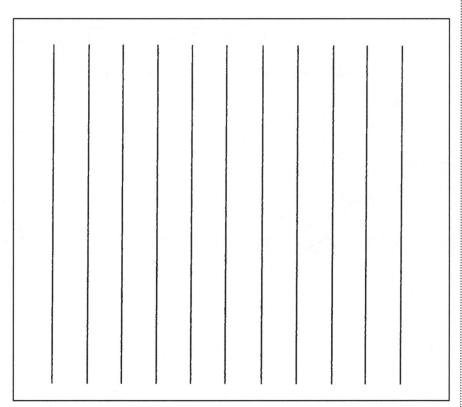

Photocopy this page four times. This makes four picture frames and four lined sheets. Cut out the four individual picture frames and four lined sheets. Attach four of each type to blank 8½" x 11" sheets to make two master sheets---one for quarter-sheet picture frames and one for quarter-sheet lined paper.

Make copies of each master sheet and cut them into fourths to produce as many quarter-sheet picture frames or lined sheets as you need for your class.

Store your half-sheet and quarter-sheet maps (next page) in painted and labeled cereal boxes (p. 35 & 56) or cake mix boxes (p. 58).

Publishing Center
Half-Sheet Map Reproducibles

Small Maps
Using small maps integrates geography & social sciences into all subjects.

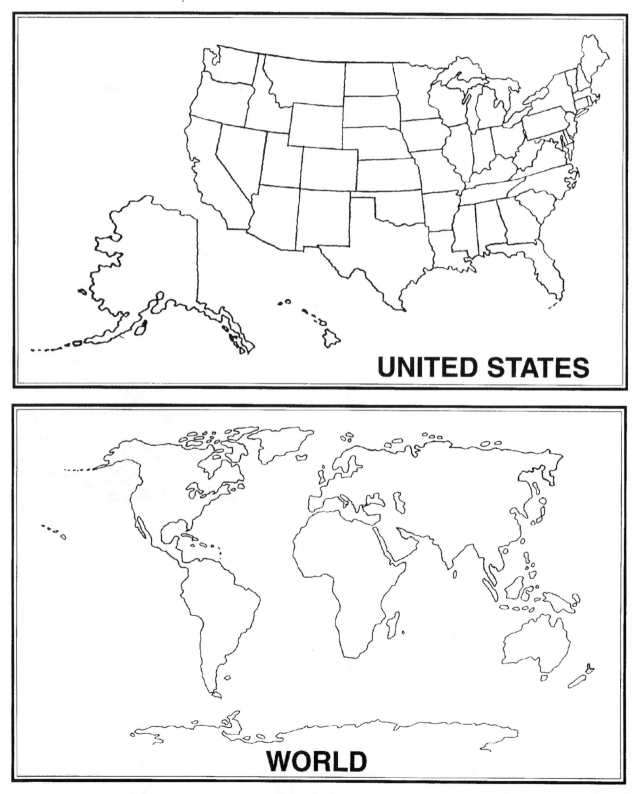

UNITED STATES

WORLD

Publishing Center
Time Line Reproducibles

Time Lines

Use time lines to help students sequence historical events, a person's life (even the student's), or a story line.

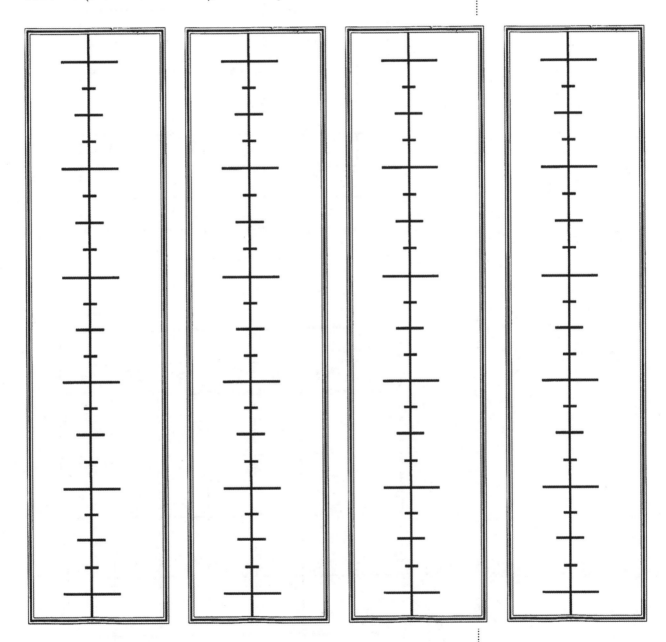

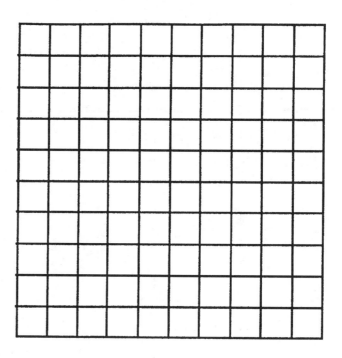

Month:						
S	**M**	**T**	**W**	**T**	**F**	**S**

Publishing Center
Helper's Wheel Reproducibles

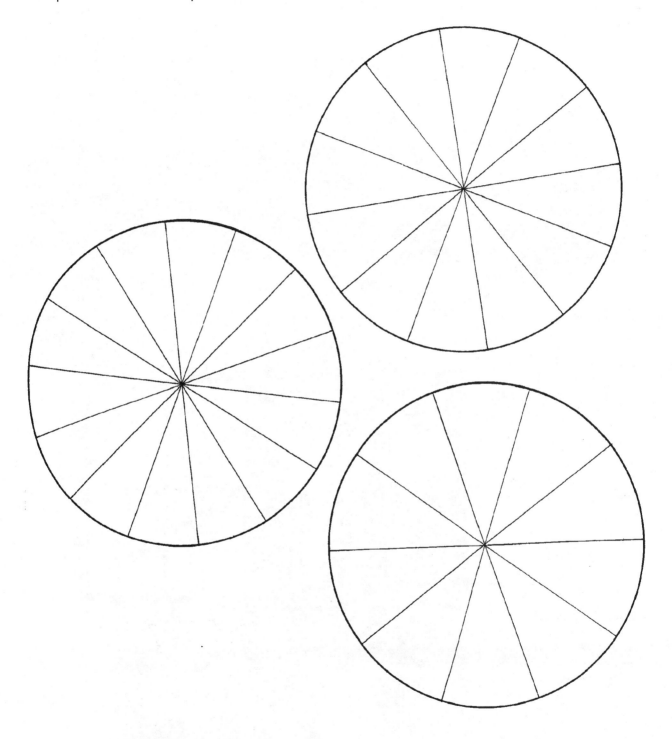

Publishing Center
Graphics

Graphic Publishing Aids

Notice the use of rain gauges and thermometers (patterns on page 143), quarter-sheets of lined paper, picture frames, and grids.
I believe in having a lot of graphic publishing aids available for student use in journals, projects, study guides, experiment stations, etc.

The Four Door Shutter Fold (above) is a Foldable™ project on sound waves and radar. It includes a timeline graphic (page 53) of the life of Chriestian Andreas Doppler, the inventor of Doppler radar,

Quarter-sheets can be stored in cake mix boxes that have been cut in half. The boxes can be painted, labeled and glued together to form a storage unit.

Publishing Center
Graphics

Example Project

This project is about one of the fifty states, and uses publishing center graphics on the front, back, and inside. If each student prepared a similar project on a different state, the class could do any of the following:

• Compare and contrast average seasonal temperatures, precipitation amounts, land area, water sources, key events, and more.

• Write word problems based upon the information recorded.

• Sort the states into categories and/or regions based upon data (such as average winter high temperature).

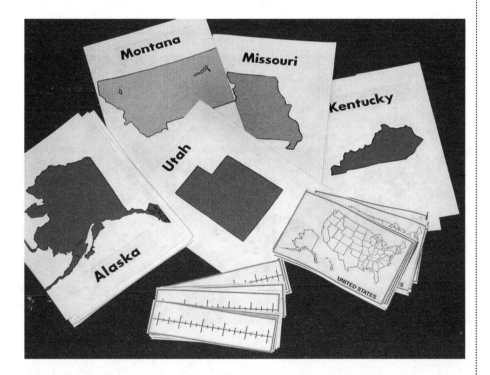

Timelines could be used with these shutterfold projects to record and present sequential information on key past and present events in each state's history. See the timeline used in the project on page 56.

Publishing Center
Graphics

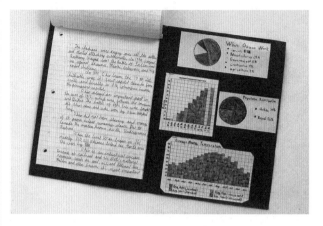

Incorporating Graphic Aids
Notice how publishing center graphics have been incorporated into this student's report (above).

Storing Graphic Aids
Photo above shows my favorite method for storing publishing center graphic aids. I collect cake mix boxes, cut them in half, and paint them or cover them with colored paper. I encourage students to use these graphic publishing aids when writing in their journals, doing daily work, taking notes, researching information, presenting reports, or developing projects. As part of an assignment, I will often require students to use publishing center graphics. For example, a report on the Civil War might require the inclusion of a map and a timeline.

Publishing Center
Scratch Paper

Collect And Use Scratch Paper

Scratch paper can be used for many projects and activities, saving schools a lot of money. To collect scratch paper, ask permission to place an empty colorful box near a photocopy machine with a sign that reads "Teacher Needs Scratch Paper." You will collect more paper than you can use. Have a parent who works in an office building collect and deliver paper to your classroom.

Note From Dinah

When I first began to teach, the cost of a ream of white copy paper was about $1.00, or $10.00 a case. Today this paper averages $35.00 to $39.00 a case, and the cost continues to rise.

• Allow young students to use scratch paper to practice cutting folded paper in half (see page 21).

• Use scratch paper to teach students a new fold or activity. As a class, practice cutting or folding scratch paper before making final projects.

• Cut scratch paper into 1/4 or 1/2 sheets, place them in the publishing center, and allow students to create their own graphics on the "clean" side of the paper. When glued onto a project the "dirty" side of the paper will not show!

• Several of my *Foldables*™ can be made using scratch paper. Example: Pyramid Fold Diorama. Fold the pyramid with the clean side of the paper to the inside and the "dirty" side to the outside as pictured (right).

Publishing Center
Templates

Templates

Templates can be purchased for use in a publishing center for writing titles, labeling, and drawing shapes.

Bound Book Templates:

When making my Bound Book Foldable using unlined paper, templates help students mark where they are to start and stop cutting. To make a classroom set of templates, laminate several brightly colored sheets of 8½" x 11" paper. Cut these laminated papers in half. As shown in the photographs, measure one inch from each end of one of the long sides, and place a mark. See Bound Book (Journal) instructions in any book from Dinah Zike's *Big Book* series.

Use the small template to make bound books out of 8½"x11" paper. Use the large template pictured when making books out of 11"x17" paper.

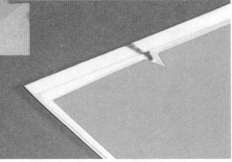

Publishing Center
Rubber Stamps & Punches

Rubber Stamps

Have inexpensive rubber stamps made for use in your publishing center. Stamps can help teachers and students organize work, communicate goals, document what work has been done, and more. For example, stamps might be used to record which draft or revision a student is working on, or for teachers to notify parents that the student's paper was "Read but not graded." Or, if a student wishes to do extra work based upon what they are learning, they might stamp a paper "Practice Makes Perfect!" This allows the teacher and parents to know that this is not the assignment, but student-generated work. Just knowing they can use a special stamp if they do extra work motivates some students to go beyond what is required.

Punches can be used to decorate student writing, and they can also be used as motivational tools or rewards.

Student Response Boards

A Classroom Set

Small, personal response boards are excellent tools for students who are practicing handwriting, participating in group drill activities, writing, spelling, studying vocabulary words, practicing

math facts, and more. The boards can be used individually by students, as group activities, or teacher-directed class activities.

Teacher-Made Chalkboards

Chalkboards (below) are easy and inexpensive to make, and can help organize the classroom to meet the individual needs of each student.

Dry erase on 2'x 4' plastic ceiling tile

Materials Needed:

• One 4' x 8' sheet of masonite cut into one-foot squares. (Ask a lumberyard representative to cut the masonite.)
• Slate black chalkboard paint (purchased or ordered from paint stores).
• Sponge brushes for painting.
• Permanent marker and ruler for drawing handwriting lines (optional).

Use sponge brushes to paint the smooth side of the masonite squares with blackboard paint. Allow paint to dry thoroughly and apply a second coat. When dry, handwriting lines can be drawn with a permanent marker. Students use the smooth, painted side of the board for writing with chalk, and the rough back for tactile writing with the tip of the finger.

Dry Erase Boards:

Use 2' x 4' x 1/8" plastic ceiling tiles (photo left) found in building supply stores to make your own dry erase boards. Use the smooth side.

Student Response Boards

Teacher-Made Magnetic Chalkboards

To make magnetic chalkboards (photo right), use thin one-foot sections of sheet metal instead of masonite. Use hot glue to mount the sheet metal on heavy cardboard that is slightly larger than the sheet metal sections. Bind the edges with several layers of strong, thick cloth tape or plastic tape to make sure no sharp edges are exposed.

Traditional Board Drill: "Say - Write - Say"

Use with small masonite chalkboards, or amend and use with dry erase boards.

• The teacher calls out a letter, number, or word to be written by the students.

• Students recite the letter, number, or word slowly, and are encouraged to visualize what they are saying.

• With chalk, students write on the chalkboard what they have visualized and said to themselves, or they write with their finger on the textured side of the masonite, saying the letter or number, or spelling the letters that form the given word as they write them.

• Students recite the letter, number, or word again after it is written.

Magnetic tape (lower photo) can be purchased in strips or precut sections at craft stores or in the craft department of larger discount stores, teacher supply stores, or art supply stores.

Making Classroom-Sized Magnetic Chalk Boards

For a classroom magnetic blackboard, use a large piece of sheet metal that has been painted with blackboard paint (upper photo) and has the edges of the metal sheet covered with several layers of strong, thick cloth tape or plastic tape. Use your imagination to design and cut response boards in different sizes and shapes.

Magnetic Boxes

Make A Magnetic Box

Paint the lids of supply boxes (photo below uses cigar boxes) with several coats of blackboard paint. For a magnetic blackboard box top, use tin-snips to cut sections of thin sheet metal slightly smaller than the top of the student supply boxes. Be careful cutting, or get help from a professional, as the edges are very sharp. It is possible that a hardware store or sheet metal shop will cut these for you if they have been given the dimensions and a few days notice. Hot glue the tin onto the lid, and bind the edges to the box using strong, heavy cloth or plastic tape. Do not allow sharp edges to be exposed.

Use a 2-inch strip of tape to reinforce the box's inside hinge line. The inside lid can be covered with felt and used as a miniature felt board. Store counting sticks, magnetic chalkboard aids, a sock for cleaning the chalkboard, chalk (can be stored inside the sock), and other supplies in the "magic" box.

Teacher Tip

Rather than making boxes for each student each year, make them for your classroom and allow students to use them for special activities. Or make only five or six and use them for small group instruction. Allow students to work on the boxes as a reward for good behavior or for special academic accomplishments.

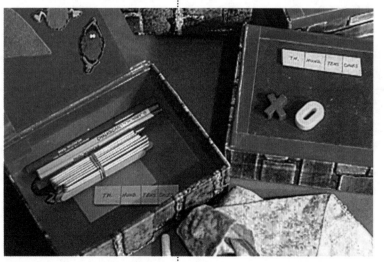

Note From Dinah

When I worked with small groups of K-6 remedial math students, they begged me to "use the boxes" when we practiced multiplication facts, worked with fractions or decimals, reviewed place value, and focused on other drill-type activities. You might allow the students to use the boxes as a reward for good behavior or as a free-time/skills-based activity.

Study Cards and Flash Cards

In And Out Of Fashion

Flash Cards: We have all used them as students and as teachers. Math fact cards were some of the first teaching aids available for the classroom. Flash cards go in and out of fashion as the pendulum of education swings.

Flash cards can be used to provide a great number of objective-based activities. They can be used in constructive ways to provide review, drill, and reinforcement of new data, and they provide hands-on activities for students.

Use Objective-Based Flash Cards For:

• "Time fillers" for the individual student or the entire class.
• Home Study. Students check them out like a library book.
• 5-minute breaks.
• Games led by the Game Show Host (see page 43).
• Practice drill and speed drill.
• Learning Center activities.
• Rainy Day activities.
• *First Thing in the Morning* or *End of the Day* activities.

Rainy Day Drill

Set up several flash card activity areas around the edge of the room or on tables. Divide the class into groups. Assign a set of cards to each group. Set a timer and allow students 4 to 5 minutes to work with the cards. At the end of the allotted time the teacher or Game Show Host Helper tells the students what to do next. For example:

Teacher/Game Show Host: "Clean the area." (Allow a short amount of time.)

Teacher/Game Show Host: "Rotate to the next station."

Begin the timer and start again. Continue until all students have had time to work in each of the stations.

Flashcards can be fun. Here you see shaped cards I used when teaching first grade.

Study Cards and Flash Cards

Store flash cards in stacked cans (see page. 34).

Making Flash Cards

Making flash cards for your classroom allows you to gear each set of cards to your students' needs. See the section on obtaining help for such tasks as making flash cards (see page 102).

Teacher Tip

Label every card according to the unit, chapter, or skill being taught. Examples: Dolch Word List A or B might be coded D-A and D-B. Vocabulary should be labeled according to the story and level. Chapters can be labeled as Sci-1 (Science Text Chapter One) or SS-14 (Social Studies Text Chapter 14).

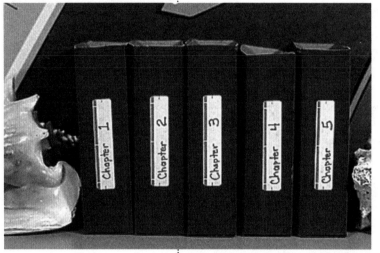

Storing Flash Cards

• Examine the different storage methods illustrated on this page and in the section "Classroom Storage" (Pages 128 - 132). Also see pages 34, 35.
• Make a flash card "library" using painted cake mix boxes (left). To see how they're made, go to page 131.
• Use die-cut machines (such as Ellison machines) to quickly make shaped cards.

Store flashcards in a cake mix box or cereal box "library."

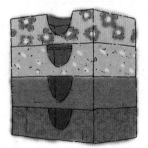

Tissue boxes that open to the side can be painted and stacked to form inexpensive, temporary, storage units.

Flash Card and Stationery Pockets

Two- And Three-Pocket *Foldables*™

Use these two- and three-pocket *Foldables*™ to store flash cards, publishing center papers, and graphics. See page 51 for quarter-sheet patterns. For additional ideas and uses, see any of the books in **Dinah Zike's Big Book of...** series and **Dinah Zike's Big Book of Word Lists: Phonics, Spelling, Vocabulary, and Grammar.**

A & B: Use 11"x17" paper to make three-pocket Foldables™.

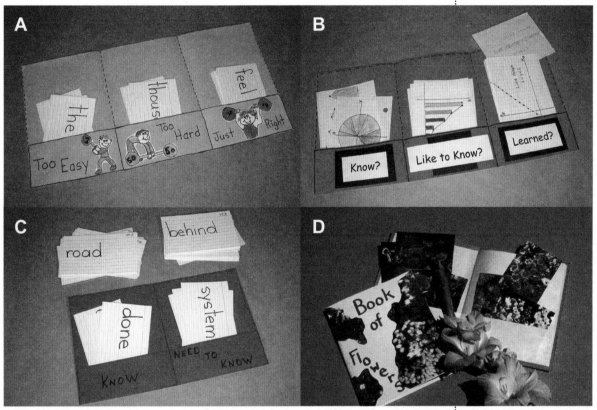

Use index cards, strips of scratch paper, or quarter sheets of note-book paper to make the cards that are stored in the pockets. Cards might be used to record research information, take class notes, make vocabulary study cards, and more.

C & D: Use 8½"x11" paper to make two-pocket Foldables™

Classroom Work Baskets

Two Sets Of Work Baskets
Place two baskets, trays, or boxes side by side. Have clean handwriting paper, task cards, worksheets, observation activities, reading materials (copies of a poem, short story, etc.), available in the left baskets. Completed assignments are placed in the baskets on the right. You could designate a Paper Helper to place the assignments in numerical order. See pages 42, Paper Helper and 39, Helping Hand.

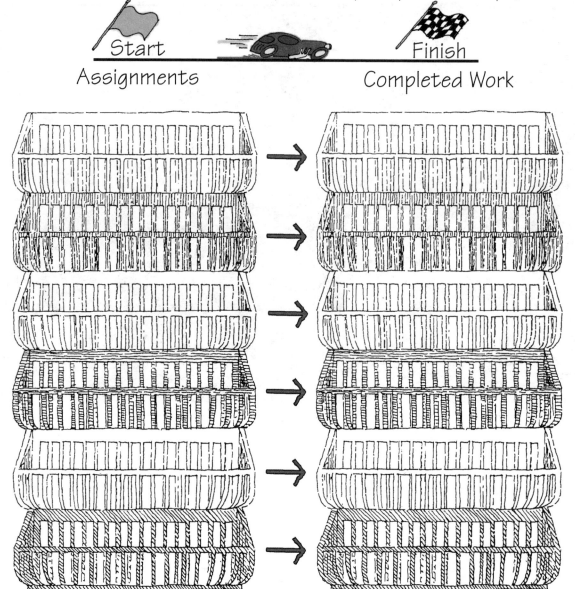

Start Assignments → Finish Completed Work

Work baskets can provide a variety of short assignments for groups or individuals. Several groups can work from the baskets at the same time, allowing other activities to take place simultaneously.

Classroom Work Baskets

Basket Setup

Student work baskets can be used for any subject, and are especially effective when a teacher works with small groups or while providing individualized instruction and conferencing.

To prevent all students from working on the same basket at the same time (making it nearly impossible for observation, reading a book, making a *Foldable*™, working on the classroom computer, studying flashcards used in the baskets), try the following procedures:

Procedures:

• Arrange the seating so that students from different groups are seated together, either at a table or in rows. Then, when the first group of students is called to come over and work with you, students come from all over the room.

• Assign a second group of students (still at their desks) to start with the top basket and work down.

• Assign a third group to start with the bottom basket and work upward to the top basket.

• If there is a fourth group, have them begin with the middle basket and work with the baskets in a pre-determined order.

• After you finish working with the first group, they return to their seats and begin with the top basket, working down.

Baskets Really Work

Students enjoy the variety that baskets provide. "Basket Work" encourages students to become responsible for finishing tasks on their own. Student progress can be readily monitored by checking the basket next to an activity. Baskets collect papers for your Paper Helper (see page 42) to organize.

Name:_____
Date:_____

Basket #1 ☐
_____
_____

Basket #2 ☐
_____
_____

Basket #3 ☐
_____
_____

Basket #4 ☐
_____
_____

Basket 5: ☐
_____
_____

I made the checklist above on my computer. Students use it to check off the baskets as they complete their work with each one. The writing lines are for personal student notes and reminders.

Hanging Student Work

Display And Collect

Using grade book numbers (page 72) and clothes pins will simplify collecting student work and expedite the grade- recording process for younger children. Each student places his/her completed work on a "clothesline" using a clothes pin that is labeled with their grade book number. A quick glance tells you who has and has not turned in their work. Your Paper Helper removes the completed work in numerical, sequential order. See pages 71, 72 on grading.

If your classroom has a lay-in grid ceiling, you can use ready-made hangers (building or office supply stores) or make your own from ordinary paper clips! (photos, right)

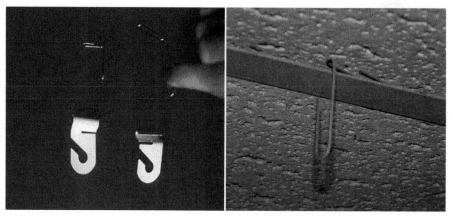

Fire Codes

Each teacher is responsible for making sure their classroom meets all fire code regulations regarding displaying paper on walls and hanging from ceiling. Before displaying student work in your classroom, call your local fire chief for information, and inquire about school fire codes.

Grades

Make It Easy On Yourself

The task of taking grades on a daily basis becomes much easier by using the following procedures. Students will learn to check and edit their work in the same way that you do, and they will obtain a better understanding of how the grading system (and accountability) works.

In the top center of a completed worksheet, have students write a letter grade that reflects how they feel they performed. This gives the teacher an idea of how students assess their own performance. The teacher writes his/her grade below the student grade. It is important to know whether or not students are realistic about their progress and performance.

Young students will enjoy grading their own papers using symbols they draw or stamp onto the top right corner of their papers:

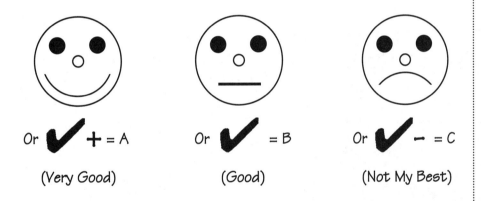

Or ✔+ = A   Or ✔ = B   Or ✔– = C

(Very Good)   (Good)   (Not My Best)

Openly discuss and clearly outline what is required to receive an A, B, C, or specific number grade. When applicable, jointly design rubrics, and demonstrate how to use them as an assessment tool. On occasion allow older students to use a graded master copy of the paper or activity they have completed to grade their own work.

Students need to feel responsible for the work they produce. They must understand that teachers do not "give" grades, and that certain conditions must be met to "earn" a grade. Self-checking, or re-evaluating, can help students become more aware of the quality of their work.

Recording Grades

Least Favorite Job

Most teachers, when asked to name their least favorite job, will quickly respond, "grading!" In most teaching jobs, this task cannot be eliminated; however, it can be less time consuming, and the process will provide more time to consider other important aspects of performance evaluation.

Numbers In A Row

Place consecutive numbers beside each student's name in the grade book. Tell each student their number, then post them in a place where all can see. If your class is departmentalized, ask students to write the period number first, followed by a hyphen and the student's number. For example, 3-14 indicates third period, student number 14.

Have the students write their number in the upper right corner on every paper they turn in.

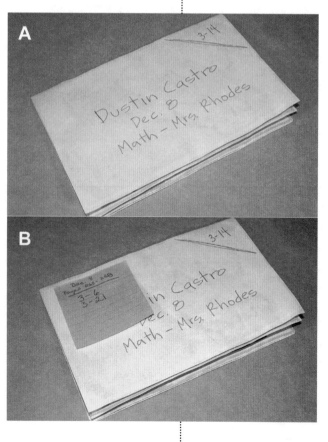

Picture And Caption

A. Have students draw a diagonal in the top right corner, forming a right triangle and write their numbers in this triangle.

Your Paper Helper (see "Classroom Jobs," page 42) places these papers in numerical order.

B. If a paper is missing, have the Helper record the number of the missing paper on a sticky-back note, and place the note/notes on the first paper. You will know at a glance who did and did not turn in their papers. Keep the notes until missing work is submitted.

Report cards can be arranged in numerical order to expedite recording.

Portfolios: Assessment & Storage

Note From Dinah

I like to keep portfolios in the classroom since they are used daily. Students retrieve journals, uncompleted work, information sheets, previously completed activities, vocabulary lists, projects, and more. When portfolios are removed from the room, there is the possibility they will not return when needed. I have seen students ask to leave the classroom in order to get a portfolio they left in their locker or their car. Sometimes students purposefully left portfolios at home so they would not have papers to work on the next day in class.

Portfolios Never Leave The Classroom

1. Use a one-gallon resealable plastic storage bag.
2. Cut off one small bottom corner to prevent the bags from holding air when sealed.
3. Using permanent marker, write student names close to the top of the bag, just below the "zipper."
4. If available, place student pictures (see page 38) next to their names. Cover the written name and/or the photocopied student photo with 2" clear tape.
5. Place a piece of cardboard (the side of a cereal box works well) inside the bag for strength and to act as a divider for student work.
6. Store the portfolios by standing the bags inside large-size (13 - 16 lb.) laundry detergent boxes (the ones that come with plastic handles).

Note: Cover the graphic side of the cereal box cardboard with duplicated sheets — maps, information sheets, math facts or formulas, key vocabulary or sight words, periodic table of elements, others.

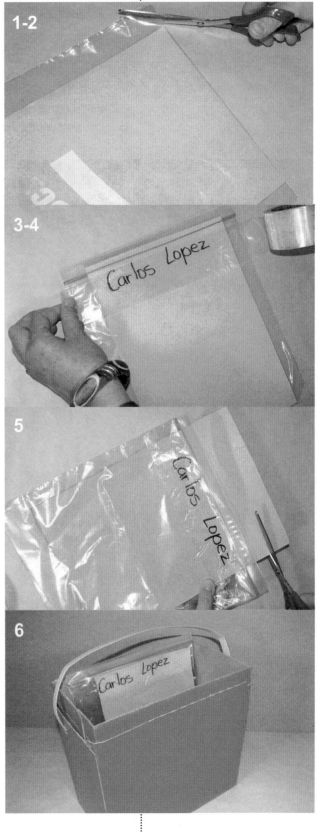

Portfolios: Assessment & Storage

Portfolios In Student Notebooks

Follow the instructions for making the plastic bag portfolios on page 73, and add a strip of 2" clear tape along the left side of the plastic bag. Using a sheet of notebook paper as a guide, punch three holes with a hole punch through the tape and the bag. This bag will now allow students to store and transport work in three-ring binders as they move to and from the classroom and home.

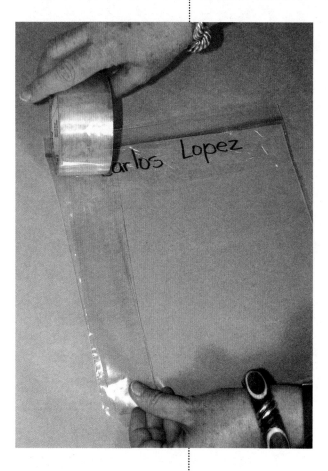 

File Folders: Assessment & Storage

Change Of Pace

For variety, have students file practice sheets, *Foldables*™, or daily work activities each day—Monday, Tuesday, Wednesday, and Thursday—in their file folder or plastic bag portfolio. Throughout the week students can correct, edit, change, or rewrite their answers before you collect the files on Thursday afternoon for grading. However, before collecting the papers, ask students to staple or clip them together and grade their work as a set. They are giving themselves a grade for how they feel they have performed for the week. Students place their grade in the top right-hand corner of the stapled stack (see pages 71, 72).

Research And Projects

When doing research and/or working on a project, it is often helpful if each student has a file folder or a pocket folder for collecting notes, pictures, graphs, print-outs of web research, interviews, articles, and more. The file folders are numbered with the student's name and number from the grade book (page 72) and stored in a labeled and painted/decorated cardboard box (photos right).

Assessment: Averaging Grades

Student Demonstration

Demonstrate to students what happens when a low grade is averaged with a high grade using the following activity.

1. Select two extremely different grades and round them off to the nearest ten. For example, 92 (90) and 51 (50).

2. Make two stacks of candy; one with 9 pieces in the stack, and the other with 5 pieces in the stack.

3. Move candies between the stacks to make the stacks as even as possible. In this example, two candies were moved from the stack of nine, leaving seven in that stack. Those two candies were added to the stack of five, making it a stack of seven.

4. This demonstrates visually to students how a grade of 50 will bring a grade of 90 down to a 70. I have heard students say, "I got an "A" on a paper last week; I'm doing fine." They do not understand how quickly an "A" can become a "C" or lower when low grades are averaged with a high grade.

5. Demonstrate how you as a teacher average grades using paper and pencil and/or a calculator: 91 + 52 = 143. 143 divided by 2= 71.5.

Assessment In General

Note From Dinah

Whole books are written on assessment. I advise new teachers to become familiar with as many assessment techniques as possible. In this book, I discuss assessment only as it relates to organization. Simply put, I find there are three main types of assessment—recognition, recall, and production. When explaining these types of assessment to students and parents, I want them to realize that most of my grades will come from production-type assessment tools such as *Foldables*™. It is not uncommon for student grades to drop when this is implemented. Students who receive grades based primarily on recognition and recall activities tend to score higher, and thus make higher grades on their report cards. However, I do not feel this is a true reflection of what they know. Frequently when students move from elementary to middle school their grades will drop because middle school usually requires more production.

Photocopied worksheets and workbooks are notorious for being predominately recognition and recall assessment tools. When there is production on these assessment tools, it is in a very simple form and very controlled by specific instructions—write a sentence about..., circle all the short "a" words on the page, compute the three-digit times two-digit multiplication problems without regrouping.

Production is a far more effective assessment tool, but more difficult and subjective to grade. When students write journal entries or a descriptive paragraph, when they write word problems based upon two of the math calculations they have just completed, when they design their own experiment to answer a question, when they do a research project on Manifest Destiny, or when they read two poems and compare the author's style and purpose, they are producing something that demonstrates their knowledge and skills as well as their weaknesses and needs.

Collect Verbs Associated With Each Type Of Assessment:

RECOGNITION	RECALL	PRODUCTION
mark	name	compare
circle	list	graph or chart
match	describe	write
select	recite	diagram

Assessment Documentation

Oral Documentation

Use audio or video tapes to record students during oral reading time or during the presentation of a project. I ask for audio tapes on the school supply list and tell parents they will be returned at the end of the year. These tapes make nice end-of-the-year presents for parents.

Written Documentation

Keep a few examples of student work throughout the year. These can be kept in files or one-gallon bags using the same process outlined for student porfolios. (See portfolios, page73.) However, these bags never leave the room, and are used for analyzing yearly progress. Eliminate stacks of paper by using a scanner to scan student work- sheets or notebook paper essays and turn them into electronic files. Parents and aides can help scan examples every week or two. When developmentally appropriate, teach students how to use the scanner so they can select and record papers they would like to include in their personal, electronic file folder. Ask students to bring a blank CD that can be used for storing student computer-generated writing, reports, and other scanned work.

Observed Behavior Documentation

Learn to record what you observe in journals. that you can refer to when needed. These notes can be referred to when needed, or shared with students, parents, and other teachers working with the child.

I used spiral journals (above) to record observations and take anecdotal notes. Parent meetings and student confer- ences were more productive when I had daily or weekly notes & examples to present.

Gummed paper was used to take observation notes, and a student chart was used to post the notes in this Early Childhood classroom I visited at Boley School, Ouachita Parish, Louisiana.

Computer Lists

Student Activity Lists

Make a list of student names in the same order as they appear in your grade book. Leave a space at the top of the page to show the activity involved. Print numerous copies of this list, and staple them together to form a pad. Check off each student's name when the activity is completed. Use the list for keeping track of money, disciplinary measures, parental visits, yearbook orders, special events, etc.

This master list helps eliminate notes made on the bottom of other papers (which are often lost), and also maintains a record of past events. For example: Which student has never bought a book from the book club? Why? Would this student like a book?

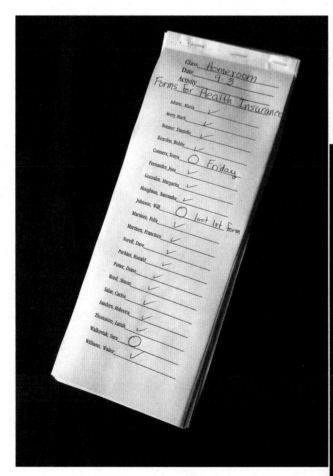

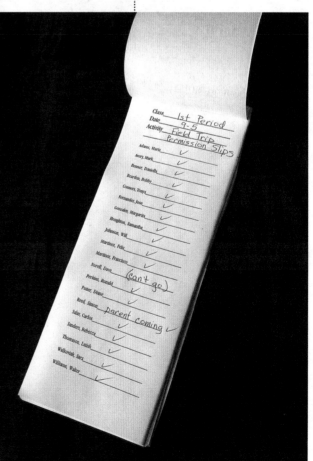

Grouping Activities

As students enter the class-room they draw a paper from the sock that will determine their group for the week. This is a neutral grouping tech-nique that is not based upon student abilities or skills. It is perfect for organizing daily activities.

Reinforcing Objectives

Every day we meet new people with whom we must learn to work and socialize. People who come into our lives—our neighbors, our boss, fellow employees, and even our relatives—cannot be hand-selected to fit our personalities. Students also must learn to work with other students. This social process can be developed in young children, and you can be an inte-gral part of the process. Initiate this with your grouping activities.

As teachers, a great deal of time is spent calling out students' names to place them in small activity groups. As you call their names, you are intentionally or unintentionally using verbal and non-verbal thoughts and actions that affect your group choic-es. Those same thoughts and actions help determine how each student reacts to being placed in a partic-ular group. Verbalizing that John and Billy cannot be in the same group because they cannot work well together is stating an expected negative behavior. John and Billy will happily verify your expectations.

Students "Pick" Their Group

As students enter the classroom on Monday morning, each one draws a piece of paper from a sock. The pieces of paper indicate the group each student will be in for the week. This works well because it creates a sense of teacher neutrality as well as expectation on the part of the student. Ensure that the student has drawn only one piece of paper.

This technique works particularly well in classrooms where the Helper's Wheel is used. Students get excited about the weekly rituals of changing jobs and changing groups on Monday morning.

Grouping Activities

How To Group And Learn

Select an educational objective, and determine how many groups are needed. For example: Your educational objective is to review the inner planets and asteroids of the solar system. Groups needed are 1) Mercury Cards, 2) Venus Cards, 3) Earth Cards, 4) Mars Cards and 5) Asteroid Belt Cards. To determine how many cards you need to put in your sock:

$$\frac{\text{NUMBER OF STUDENTS}}{\text{NUMBER OF GROUPS}} = \begin{array}{c}\text{NUMBER OF DRAW CARDS}\\ \text{NEEDED WITH SAME SYMBOL}\\ \text{FOR EACH GROUP}\end{array}$$

Twenty-six students divided by five groups could form four groups of five and one group of six. Therefore you would need 5-card sets for Mercury, Venus, Earth, and Mars, and one 6-card set for Asteroids.

Daily Activities Include:

- Any student living on Mars can go get a drink of water.
- If you live on the second planet from the Sun you may sharpen your pencil.
- If you live on the Water Planet go to the "Check It Out!" center.
- Planetoids, go to reading circle.
- Teacher stands in the door and says, "I am the Sun. Please line up in order of your orbits from the Sun." Students then line up in the following order: Mercury, Venus, Earth, Mars, and Asteroid Belt.

These activities reinforce fun facts, new concepts, and vocabulary terms during routine classroom activities. They will also encourage higher thinking level skills as you ask more challenging questions that require analysis. You will be amazed at how much students learn and at how much you need to know to keep these grouping activities challenging for your students during one week's time. This becomes a learning process for teacher and students.

Grouping Activities

Post It

It is sometimes helpful to make a poster with all your student's names listed. Leave a space beside each name for tacking or taping the grouping card selected from the sock (see page 80). The Poster reminds students of who is in each group, and helps them learn selected objectives. Use this same grouping activity throughout the week in all subject areas.

Hints For Attaching Grouping Cards

• Display the poster on a cork board and use push pins.
• Laminate a posterboard chart and attach the grouping cards with tape.
• Use self-adhering notes or double-sided tape to attach grouping cards to a laminated chart.

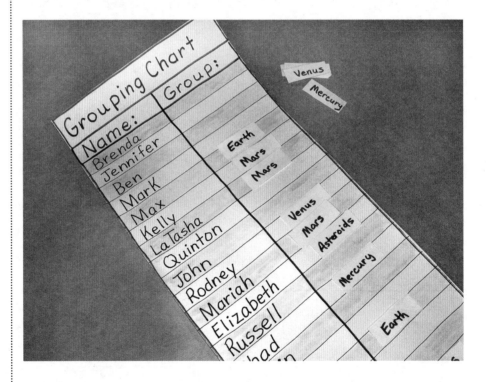

Grouping Activities

Objectives To Be Taught Or Reinforced

Select educational objectives to be used for grouping during the week. Review these examples and then create your own.

• **Numbers:** If students have drawn numbers from the "grouping sock," the teacher calls out an equation or inequality students must solve before they may line up. If the numbers drawn were "10", "15", "20", "25", and "30" to form five groups, the teacher might say, "If you are the answer to 15+5, you may line up." Or, the teacher might say, "If you are greater than 26, but less than 31, you may line up."

• **Consonants:** If students have drawn the consonants "t", "s", "j", and "w" to form four groups, the teacher calls out words that begin or end with the featured consonants (depending on what skill is being stressed) to tell students when to line up. For example, if a student drew the letter "w", they would not line up until the teacher called a word beginning (or ending) with the "w" sound.

• **Vowels:** Follow the same procedure used for consonants.

• **Blends:** Follow the same procedure used for consonants.

• **Prefixes & Suffixes:** Follow the same procedure used for consonants.

• **Animal Classification:** Students draw the following cards to form five groups: fish, amphibians, reptiles, birds, mammals. The teacher might say, "If you breathe through gills, you may line up now." Or, "If you lay eggs and have feathers, you may line up now." Note, if the teacher had said, "If you lay eggs, you may line up now.", students who had drawn fish, amphibian, reptile, and bird cards could have lined up.

Lining Up

Competition At Both Ends

Being first in line—any line—can become a game for students. They each want to be considered special, and being first in line is a way to gain special attention. On the other end of the spectrum, some students will take three-inch steps to get to the line last. There are several ways to make this daily routine less competitive.

Leader Always First

Choose a weekly Classroom Leader using the Helper's Wheel. This student is always first in line (see page 42).

Line Up By Groups

Have students line up by the groups they are working in for the week. (See grouping activities on page 80.) Review the following pre-school example used to teach and reinforce knowledge of four colors, the circle shape, and ordinal and cardinal numbers 1-4: From the Grouping Sock students drew green, blue, red, and yellow circles at the beginning of the week to form four groups. The teacher might say, "Green circles line up, after the leader, blue circles, second; red circles, third, yellow circles fourth, at the end of the line."

Line Up Randomly

Have students line up at random, and ask them to note their number in line—first, second, third, etc. The teacher then draws a number from a jar containing a number for each student. The student whose number is chosen is allowed to do something special that day. (There may be several students who have "won" by the end of the day.)

Use academic, objective-based "prizes," such as free time in a Learning Center, flash cards to take home for a day, special books to take home or read in the room, free time in the science center, time for using the microscopes or computer, and many others.

Show & Share

Objects Brought For Sharing

The morning is your busiest time of day. Numerous housekeeping responsibilities must be fulfilled before your daily academic routine can begin. Unfortunately, this is also the time when students need your personal attention the most.

Students bring all kinds of unusual objects for sharing. They want the teacher and their fellow students to see these treasures immediately!

This student *brought* an armadillo fetus to school in a jar of alcohol. The mother armadillo was killed by a car and the child saw the dead baby near the mother's body. The child's mother helped her preserve it for the teacher by placing it in rubbing alcohol. (Follow your district's policy on toxic substances in your classroom.) The student had observed her teacher use this preservation method numerous times in class. (See page 140.)

Check It Out!

Problem

It's morning. LaTasha comes to school excited and ready to share a new experience. She walks into the classroom with a seashell retrieved on a family vacation, anxious to show it to you and the class. However, you are busy. You accept the seashell and place it aside, promising LaTasha that the class will view it during science.

Your day gets busier and seems even more hectic than usual. It is time for science and the study of seeds. In your rush to cover the content outlined for the day's lesson, you forget your promise to LaTasha.

But, LaTasha did not forget. She reminds you of the seashell at the most inconvenient times. Again, you must delay viewing the seashell. "We will look at it right before we go home."

Time passes quickly, and the day begins to wind down. As the students line up, get their personal belongings together, and are reminded of homework assignments, LaTasha reminds you of your promise.

Grabbing the seashell, you dash around the room, up and down the bus lines, showing the children the seashell brought early in the day.

Upon finishing this race, you hand the shell back to LaTasha with these words: "Thank you for bringing this to share with us! We enjoyed it SO MUCH!"

Here's What Really Happened:

☹ LaTasha has not been rewarded for taking an interest in sharing experiences with the class, and she has learned nothing new about her seashell.

☹ The seashell was not used as a stimulus for learning or writing.

☹ No observations or discovery experiences have taken place.

Check It Out!

Get The Students Involved

Instead of placing the seashell aside in the morning, view it with interest and a smile. Make an announcement that LaTasha has brought a seashell to share with the class. This takes about thirty seconds.

Have LaTasha place the shell on a "Check It Out!" table. This small area of the room can be a plastic table, old end table, or a strong, cardboard box painted and turned bottom up.

During the morning, tell LaTasha one or more interesting facts about the shell. Perhaps LaTasha already knows something about the shell that she would like to share. (As the students become familiar with this process, they start researching items before bringing them to school so they will have fun facts to share!) It is important that students be given full responsibility for whatever they bring to share.

LaTasha's classmates are now responsible for asking her about the seashell. Inquiries can be made during non-instructional time – lunch, breaks, P.E., etc. As students finish their work and have extra time, they can go to the *Check It Out!* table for a given amount of time to observe the objects displayed there.

"Check It Out" Tips

✔Place a one-minute timer on the table to regulate observation time. A great deal of concentrated observing can take place in a minute.

✔Always have several magnifying glasses on the table to encourage closer qualitative observations.

Check It Out!

The Check It Out Technique Has Several Advantages:

✔ It takes very little of your valuable time.

✔ Students feel important.

✔ Students develop oral language skills through questioning and answering.

✔ Students become teachers.

✔ The class has an opportunity to experience something new or different.

Discourage:

✘ Materialistic items such as CD players, clothes, and toys.

Encourage:

If you have had trouble with Show and Tell activities, consider replacing them with "Check It Out!" activities.

✔ Nature items (leaves, grass, rocks, shells, soil samples, tree bark, fossils).

✔ Living objects for observation (plant or animal). Animals are to be kept for one day of observation and then returned to the same location in which they were originally found. NOTE: Always follow school policies regarding plants and animals in classrooms.

✔ Books (fiction or nonfiction).

✔ Objects from other countries or cultures.

✔ Current event information.

✔ Objects from home that relate to topics studied in class.

✔ Math manipulatives or examples of math concepts as they are used in the student's world. For example, a student might bring an advertisement with fractions or percentages.

✔ Student inventions or investigations.

✔ Student-generated art.

✔ More!

Check It Out!

Decrease Loss And Theft

Students who would normally not steal are often tempted to do so by small, interesting objects, especially when the objects are loose in a container, and it would not be immediately obvious that one of the objects had disappeared. I have found that students will justify their atypical behavior by thinking that they will use the item, and that they need it more than the teacher/class since there are still many of the same item left in the container. Besides, they may believe no one will ever know.

I have found that when objects are stored in a designated space, and are possibly even numbered, a removed piece from the space will be obvious. For example, notice how the magnifying glasses are stored in the Check It Out! center (right). This technique helps organize a classroom and decreases loss and theft.

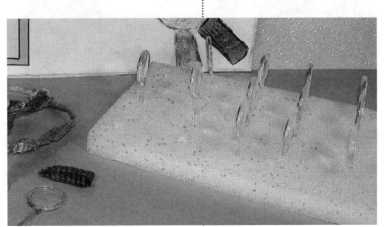

Pass It Around

Lesson Plans For Discovery And Observation

There is limited time for presenting a lesson. Objects that students need to observe and that are vital to understanding the lesson are often passed around the classroom for viewing by students.

As educators, we want to encourage discovery and questioning in the daily lesson plans; but with limited instruction time this is impossible to achieve while students pass an object around the room. Students tend to become involved with the object, and do not hear what is discussed. Or, they keep the object longer than is necessary, preventing others from seeing it before the lesson is complete.

The process can be rushed with questions such as, "Where is the object?", "Do you still have it in this row?", "Have you seen the object in the back of the room?", "Who is taking so long?", "We don't have all day now, pass that thing along!"

While your comments may help speed up the passing of the object, they also negate the true purpose in the first place; which is observing and experiencing. In addition, we then ask for scientific analysis at the same time students are playing hot-potato with the object.

Instead, try the *Take a Look at This* activity on the next page.

Take a Look at This!

Tomorrow's Lesson Today

Why wait until the day of the lesson to introduce the object to be studied? Establish a small area, and make a sign that reads, "Take A Look At This" or "Investigate This Before (Day)", in order to display items that will be discussed in future classes.

Place these objects on the table several days before the lesson that incorporates them into the curriculum. Encourage observation during different periods of the day and during free time. Again, keep individual timers and magnifying glasses on the table. Have a sign stating how many students are allowed in the observation area at one time.

When the time comes to study the object in class, the object can be passed quickly for review, since students have previously spent quality time observing and experiencing it up close.

Give your students several days to examine objects before discussing them in class. Laminate the sign, leaving a blank space for a date. Using an overhead marker or dry erase marker, write in the day the object or objects will be discussed. It is now the students' responsibility to view the object before the deadline.

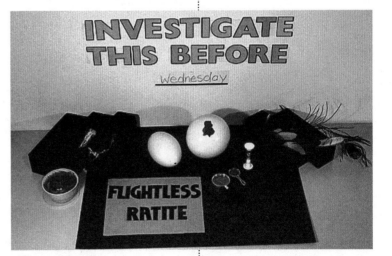

Give very young students a full week to view and experience the object before discussing it in class the next week.

Take a Look at This!

Heavy Traffic

Place "Take a Look at This!" (and/or "Check It Out!") tables in heavy traffic areas where most students pass at least a few times a day. Even the student who never gets a solid minute of viewing time will see objects longer if they are displayed on the table. Keep a magnifying glass on the table to encourage observation and discovery.

De-escalate Conflicts

Students who have personal conflicts in class can often solve their problems through sharing a new experience at the "Take A Look At This!" table. Send the fussing or tussling students to this station for an interactive "Time Out."

Use these areas as rewards or as special treats for students who have been working diligently.

Give a break to the student who seems momentarily frustrated by a difficult task or a writing assignment. Send the student to the "Take A Look At This!" Table for a one-minute break, and hopefully they will go back to work with a fresh perspective.

Like Magic

On occasion, try hiding an object being discussed until a special moment. Then make it appear as if by magic. This technique can be fun on occasion, but do not sacrifice observation and experience for the surprise factor.

Everyone Works and Shares

Keeping Track

Some students have something to share every time you ask a question or conduct a discussion. Other students will never share without being coaxed to do so. Try the following activity to make sure all students share equally. This activity is not practical for use during the entire day, but it helps the teacher and students keep track of who has and has not shared over a period of time when students are presenting projects, reading a selection, reporting on a book, and presenting special assignments.

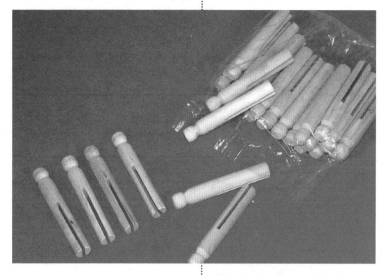

Wooden push-type clothes pins (above) are even easier to use than the spring-type (left). Note the blue paper circles and rectangles glued to the shelf cover for easy organizing.

1. Use a permanent marker to write student names or numbers on old-fashioned wooden push clothes pins or spring-type pins.
2. Place the pins around the edge of a container such as a tin coffee can or a small, square box.
3. As students share they remove their pin and place it in the can. Everyone in class can immediately see who has and has not shared.

Junk Box Art & Stress Release

Creative Expression

Decorate a box for collecting junk materials for art objects. Students can contribute "throw-away" items to the Junk Box. When they have free time from studies, or need a diversion to relieve stress, they can use the box to create their own unique "art" projects.

Examples Of Junk Box Materials:

 Small boxes from household items.

 Empty thread spools.

String, yarn, thread.

Plastic containers.

Scraps of cardboard, construction paper, foam rubber, etc.

Small pieces of wood and plastic.

Junk Box Supplies

Provide tape, glue, scissors and other supplies for constructing student creations.

Home Survey

Getting Help

If one picture is worth a thousand words, then one physical object to show in the classroom must be worth at least a hundred lectures. Physical objects add so much to the discovery process, providing the hands-on experience needed to illustrate the point under discussion.

Wish List

Have you ever wished you had unusual items to display, as well as interesting people to share experiences with your students throughout the school year? Those items and people exist, and are probably more accessible than you might think. During the second or third week of school, send a Home Survey sheet to parents, stating what units and/or topics the class will study, and asking for materials or people to facilitate those studies.

Anticipate your needs in various subjects. And remember no one will know what you need unless you tell them.

NOTE: See page 96 for an example of a form letter.

Ask parents and relatives to share:

• Personal experiences for the class on a tape recorder, video camera, CD, or DVD—a living history, a description of a trip, etc.
• Favorite books or poems--read and record.
• Employment (community helpers and volunteers, transportation workers, artists, scientists, doctors, musicians, etc.).
• Hobby or craft to share with the class.
• Gardening or an interest in plants—African violets, orchids, vegetables, antique roses, fruit tree grafting, others.
• Animals—what kind? Are they work related? Pets? Exotic?
• Collections to bring and discuss (stamps, coins, African art, old photographs, animal figurines, etc.).
• Sports (anything from football to karate).
• Food & Cooking (food from other lands, nutrition, etc.).
• Tapes, CD's, instructional videos.
• Musical instruments, art prints, classical music CD's, etc.).
• Computer equipment or technological expertise.
• Items from other states or countries.

Home Survey Form (Sample)

We need your help! Our class is taking a survey of parents and guardians to find people interested in helping with classroom projects. By filling out the Survey Form, we can determine who has items of interest or things to share with our class. Don't worry if you can't help this semester; we will send another form in January! Thanks in advance!

Mrs. Mason's Second Grade Class

Do you have a special rock, mineral, or fossil that you could share with our science class in September?

_____
_____
_____

We will be studying *Community Helpers* (all professions are important and of interest) the second six weeks. Would you share your profession with our class? If so, please tell us what you do and how to get in touch with you.

_____
_____
_____

During our morning reading block, we need parents to listen to students read and help students with spelling and vocabulary activities.
Could you work in our classroom one morning a week? One morning a month? One morning this semester?

_____
_____
_____

Do you have any unwanted magazines on the following topics that you would donate to the classroom?
_____gardening_____archaeology_____natural history

In December, we will study holiday traditions from cultures around the world. If you or your parents were born in another country; if you speak a second language; if you have traveled to other lands; or if you are familiar with other cultures, please let us know. We might ask for your help as we plan our unit of study.

_____
_____

Name of Parent or Guardian:_____
Contact Phone Number and/or E-mail:_____
_____

Communicating & Networking

Business Cards

As professionals, teachers need business cards. Determine what information you would like on the card, and either make them using your computer, or have them printed. Be sure to include the best time to contact you, such as an "off-period" or a "conference" period.

Newsletters

Get students involved in writing, designing, and publishing a weekly, bi-weekly, or monthly newsletter. Include photographs of students in action, student-made bulletin boards, student projects, and school events. Encourage students to be journalists by writing and submitting articles, poems, short stores, riddles, jokes, recipes, and sport reports for possible publication. Newsletters can be written and sent electronically via email, or they can be part of a classroom website.

Web Sites

Many teachers create websites that can be visited by parents and guardians. This is a great place to post information on skills being studied, assignments due, and events taking place.

E-Mail Address

You might have a special e-mail address where parents and guardians of students can communicate with you directly. (Most school districts provide this.) Sometimes it is helpful to have parent/teacher communication in writing.

Textbooks On-Line

When this is available, inform parents of this service and take time to explain how the texts can be accessed from home computers. This service will prevent students from having to lug heavy books home every night, and/or if students forget to take a book in which they have questions to answer or reading to complete, they can complete assignments by using the on-line text.

Collect Effectively

Get Organized

Many useful items are thrown away every day. A short note to parents may help you collect items for your classroom. This also allows parents to feel involved in their child's education. Photocopy the forms below, and fill them out. They can then be cut out and given to your students to take home. They can also be scanned and emailed to parents.

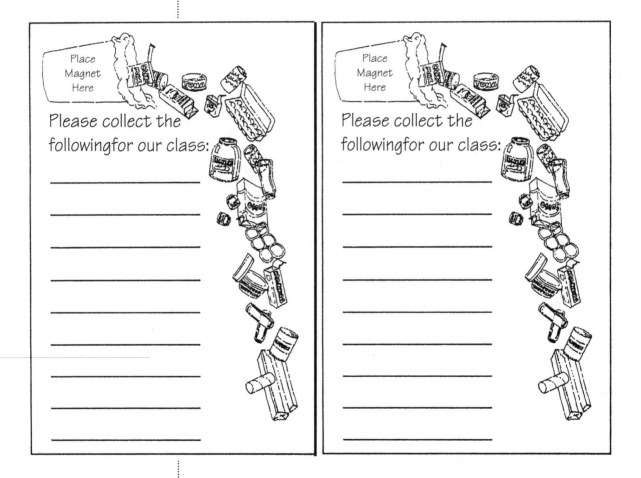

Place
Magnet
Here

Please collect the
followingfor our class:

This is a good size for displaying on a refrigerator or family note board. As an art project, make a special refrigerator magnet for students to take home and use to display the notes. Students like being part of the collection process, and they will enjoy using what is collected.

Garage Sales & Flea Markets

Reconnaissance

Find garage sales in your neighborhood that advertise materials you want for your classroom. Visit the sale, and price the objects. If you feel they cost more than you can afford, get the name and number of the owner, note what you are interested in purchasing, and call them back later to see if the item is still available. Ask if they have anything left that they are willing to donate or sell at a reduced price.

NEVER provide or discuss personal information (nor your school's information) with a stranger. You contact the seller, don't have the seller contact you.

Safety in Numbers

Always go to unknown locations with friends, and take a cell phone. A great find is not worth taking a personal risk. If you do not feel comfortable in an area or going to a certain garage sale, do not go at all!

Those Magic Words

Many times the owner, upon hearing the words "teacher" and "classroom," will offer to sell items at a reduced price, and sometimes will cheerfully donate them to your class.

Want Ads

Check the Classifieds

A proven way to collect inexpensive or unusual items, usually at no cost, is through advertising in a community or city newspaper classified section. Start the ad with a catch phrase, such as "TEACHER NEEDS..." Believe it or not, the citizens of your community know you are overworked and underpaid, and will respond in kind.

Do Not Be Afraid To Ask!

Try obtaining some of the following items through your ad:
- Magazines relating to topics you are teaching
- Used furniture for the classroom:
   - bar stools
   - book shelves
   - roll carts
- Pots and pans, hot plate
- Children's books
- Old crayons and school supplies
- Pictures or postcards
- Set of encyclopedias, encyclopedias on CD
- Microscope sets
- Radio, tape recorder, CD player, DVD and VHS player
- Video Camera, digital camera
- Computers, reference CD's, educational CD's

This newspaper ad was used successfully to collect the following: travel, science and news magazines, ten fossils of bi-valves and uni-valves, a pheasant egg and a quail egg, two file cabinets, and seven sets of bookcases.

Neighborhood Scavenger Hunt

A Neighborly Act

Conduct a **Scavenger Hunt** in your neighborhood! Notify neighbors of the materials you need for your classroom by sending them a letter or placing a notice on their doors. Provide a collection point for the items they are contributing. I keep a red toy box in front of my house for donated items. See the sample Scavenger Hunt letter below.

Date:

Scavenger Hunt

Dear Neighbor,

My _____ grade class is collecting items listed below for our classroom. If you have any of these items, or other useful items that you would like to contribute, please place them in our collection box located at: _____
_____. This collection will continue until _____.

Thanks for your help and support.
Best Wishes,

_____

Items Needed:

_____   _____   _____

_____   _____   _____

_____   _____   _____

_____   _____   _____

Getting Help

Volunteers

Often as teachers, we think it is easier to do things ourselves rather than take the time to find help. Some teachers feel that they must do everything themselves in order to be "professional". After all, who will perform these tasks in the same manner as they would?

There are people you know and trust in your community who want to feel needed and useful. Many of them would enjoy helping a teacher directly in their classroom. Others might want to make things at home and bring them to the classroom. **Check your school's rules and security procedures. Most schools require "visitors" to sign in and be recognized upon every visit. Some schools run security checks before allowing parents or community volunteers to work in classrooms.**

NO VOLUNTEERS?
A few districts have adopted policies forbidding anyone, even parents, from working in classrooms with students. Do you agree or disagree with this? What would you do if you were a teacher or a parent in one of these districts?

Help Outside the School

- Reading & audiotaping chapters in the textbooks, poems, short stories, fables, tales, etc.
- Using the computer to research topics and print articles that might be used in class.
- Making picture and reference files for upcoming projects.
- Preparing materials needed for art projects or science experiments.
- Grading practice activities or simple daily work.
- Helping to make manipulatives, bulletin boards, chalkboards, or other teaching aids.

Help Inside The School

- Reading to students, and listening to students read.
- Telling stories and/or listening to students' stories.
- Supervising science experiments and experiences.
- Practicing vocabulary, spelling words, math facts, and more.
- Summarizing or outlining key concepts and textbooks for slow readers.

Getting Help

Adoption: Not for Children Only

In communities and neighborhoods all over the country, assisted living homes and retirement homes are filled with people interested in and capable of helping with classroom activities. Adopt Classroom Grandmothers and/or Classroom Grandfathers.

Visit a local nursing home or extended-care facility and talk to the director about people who might be interested in helping. You will probably find many people who have been involved in education who would love the opportunity to help you and your students. There are many tasks they can perform to help you and your class.

It's Worth It

The most difficult part of this organizational technique is getting materials to and from the "grandparents." The most enjoyable aspect is getting the help from people who are interested in investing their time, talents, energy, and expertise in the process of education.

Invite Them To Visit

If possible invite the "grandparent(s)" to visit your classroom. They will be grateful to see the utilization of the items they helped create, grade, record, etc. Many nursing homes or assisted living centers will transport the "grandparents" to school for lunch or for a party with the students.

Give Back

Encourage your students to draw pictures, and write letters and thank you notes to the Classroom Grandparents. Have a box or basket available in which to collect these items, and do not forget to take them to the "grandparents" when you collect or deliver work.

Getting Help

Clubs, Church Groups And Colleges
Visit a community club, local business, college education class, senior citizen group, or the senior class of a church, synagogue, or mosque, and ask them to "adopt" your class. There are many tasks they can perform to help out (see page 102). Their work may be picked up at a future date, and/or often a member of the group will deliver items to the school office.

Upper Elementary, Junior High And High School Groups
Older elementary students in higher grades enjoy helping younger students. The responsibility is good for all involved. The older students begin to feel like teachers, and a bond develops between students across grade levels. Sometimes this is the most difficult form of help to organize, and it can be the least dependable. But the rewards, as you will see, are tremendous. It is worth the effort.

The "Big Book" pictured was made for this teacher and her first grade class by junior high students.

Other Volunteers
People who sit with the elderly or ill may be interested in helping a teacher cut, color, print, grade, read, and create materials for a classroom. Call hospitals or nursing centers for recommendations of people with such jobs.

Fold-away Teaching Aids

Fabric And Plastic

Teaching aids made from fabric, oil cloth, vinyl, or plastic can be used year after year. When possible, use these materials instead of poster board to create flexible, durable instructional aids that do not have to be laminated. These aids can be stepped on, written on (with an overhead projector marker or dry erase marker), folded, and stored easily!

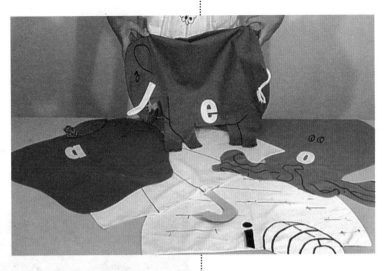

I made the fabric vowel teaching aids pictured above when I taught first grade. They were used in my classroom for two years and other classrooms for over fifteen years. I still own and use the vinyl U.S. map pictured. It is at least 20 years old.

This vinyl map of the United States offers hands-on experience and stores easily in Unit Boxes (pages 157 - 159). Use sheet vinyl to make maps, puzzles, letters, numerals, etc. Colored vinyl scraps can be obtained from car and furniture upholstery shops, sign shops, or purchased at fabric stores.

Folding *Foldables*™ Teaching Aids

Note From Dinah

Those of you who are familiar with my *Foldables*™ know that I design paper and poster board teaching aids that can be folded and stored without taking up a lot of room. Observe the *Foldables*™ on this page, and look for other examples of my *Foldables*™ on throughout this book.. (See index for locations.) .

Using Bulletin Boards

An Integral Part Of Your Classroom

Bulletin boards should be an integral part of your classroom. They display what is being studied, provide a place for posting student work, add color and excitement to the curriculum, and become interactive areas for student involvement.

Fabric vs. Paper

Try using fabric to cover a bulletin board. This can be used year after year and is easily folded and stored. It also is easier to hang and does not fade as rapidly as paper.

Seal It

After completing a bulletin board, cover it with a thin sheet of clear vinyl cut to size. Clear vinyl can be purchased at fabric stores or in the fabric departments of discount stores. Vinyl protects the materials on display, and can be written on with a dry marker or an overhead projector marker, creating another instructional center.

Mapping Destinations

When maps are covered with clear vinyl, they become visual aids that can be written on: Routes of travel can be traced, cities marked, land formations noted, distances between cities calculated, and more.

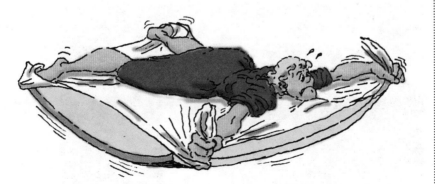

Clear vinyl easily covers large maps, bulletin boards, table tops and many other items to provide students with an erasable writing surface that keeps the covered items clean and turns them into reusable teaching tools. See "Write Here," page 33.

Permanent Bulletin Boards

Use Year After Year

Fabric cutting boards make excellent folding bulletin boards that can be used year after year. Paint the board front and back with several coats of latex enamel paint.

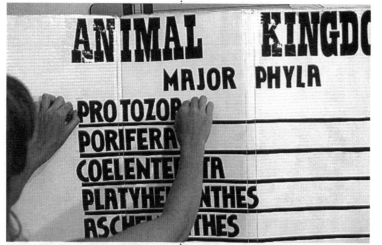

This fabric cutting board has been painted with white latex enamel paint. The words are applied with 2" clear tape. This permanent bulletin board will be used by students for classification activities.

Colored foamboard can be purchased at art supply and craft stores. These 1/4" thick boards usually come in sizes 20" x 30" and come in a variety of colors.

Mount lettering or pictures on this bulletin board with the 2" tape discussed later on page 117. Colored tape can be used to divide the board into sections. Thumb tacks, brass brads, Velcro™, and magnetic strips can be used on this board.

The board stands and makes a clever learning center backdrop. It can also be cut in half, forming two three-sectioned panels, making room divider bulletin boards.

Use permanent bulletin boards for the following:
- Timelines
- Grouping activities
- Classification activities
- Math drill and skill activities
- Spelling and/or vocabulary words
- Current event boards, and more

Shaped Bulletin Boards

For Teachers Only
Use a saw to cut shapes out of pegboard, or masonite, and use them to make unusual bulletin boards. Keep saws away from students.

Use a hobby or utility knife to cut shapes out of insulation board (lumber yard) or 4' x 8' sheets of corrugated plastic. (Look in the business phone directory under "Plastics, Distributors." Also check with any sign company. They use corrugated plastic to make inexpensive outdoor signs.) Remember, keep all knives away from students.

How To Make Them
The bear, turtle, and dinosaur bones pictured on this page were made using this process:
• Use an illustration or photo from a magazine, book, etc., or make your own illustration.
• Place the artwork in an opaque projector, and project it onto the board.
• Trace over the projected picture onto the board using a permanent marker. You can draw just the outline of the shape or get as detailed as you want to, like the T. rex skull below.
• Cut out the new artwork using a utility knife.

Chart Paper Bulletin Boards

Confessions Of A Chart Paper Tablet Hater

I confess! I hate chart paper tablets! The very first thing I bought as a teacher was a chart stand and a chart paper tablet. Then came the problems. The chart paper tablet was big and bulky. It had to go on the rickety stand that took up too much space in my classroom. It was unweildy when I tried to locate the chart I needed. The flipped pages tended to fall back in place over the chart I was trying to show my students! Then the whole thing would fall off the stand.

Like the other little problems I faced in my classroom, I wrote this one down on an index card. You can see my solution to the problems of chart paper tablets on the next page. I started using this technique in 1974, and now I see it used in classrooms all over the United States.

The main problem with chart paper tablets is mobility. I wanted to be able to take one chart and hang it somewhere or take it for a small group activity or an outdoor study session, etc. I didn't want to take the whole tablet; and if I tore out one of the chart pages, it was too flimsy to hang by itself. I found a wire clothes hanger, attached the chart paper sheet to it, and suddenly my chart was mobile! I could literally take that chart anywhere, and I could hang it anywhere.

Wrap a 2" piece of clear tape around the top of the hanger, and use it to label the chart paper. Write on the tape with a dry-erase or water-based marker. That way if you replace the chart paper bulletin board on the hanger with another one, you can easily erase and change the label.

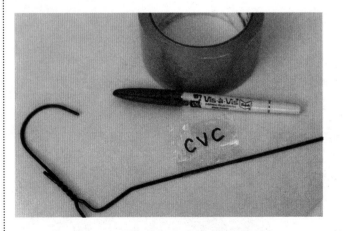

Chart Paper Bulletin Boards

Making A Chart Paper Bulletin Board

All you need is a wire clothes hanger and a stapler:

a. Fold the corners of a sheet of chart paper down at an angle leaving a straight 10" edge in the center of the paper.
b. Place a clothes hanger on top of the 10" edge.
c. Fold the 10" edge over the clothes hanger.
d. Staple the edge around the hanger. You can first put a line of glue inside the fold, but it's not necessary.

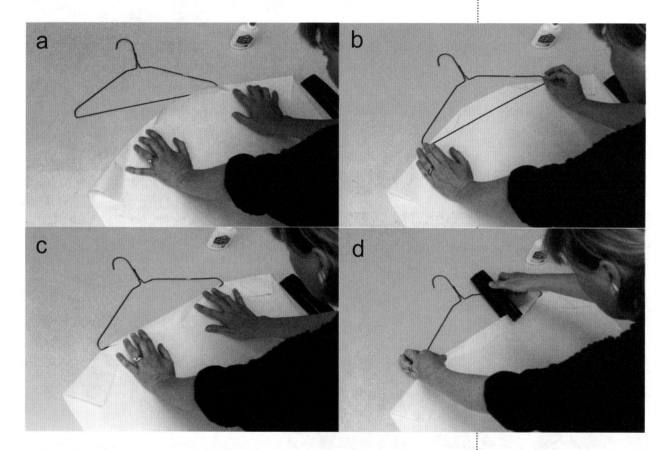

Add a label on the hanger (preceeding page). Now you have a mobile bulletin board that you can hang anywhere and take anywhere. Put a coat hook in a good spot in your classroom, and hang all your hanging bulletin boards on it. Pick out the one you need by reading the labels, and put that one out front for the class to see. If you need to show more than one at a time, put up more coat hooks.

Cubicles & Display

Cardboard Cubicles

Cut cardboard boxes or fabric cutting boards to form displays or student cubicles. You can also buy ready-made folding display boards at craft shops and art supply stores.

Make three-fold cubicles for desks or individual work areas using a fabric cutting board. Cut the board in half perpendicular to the folds, and you've produce two cubicles!

Use the following on the Cubicles:
• Sticky-back note reminders.
• Plastic sheet covers that papers can be slipped into and removed from at a future date.
• Adhesives that allow objects to be placed on and removed from the display.
• Loops of ribbon that can be used to hold pencils or pens.

Use the Cubicles for individual student needs, such as:
• Sight words or vocabulary terms.
• Writing progress check lists.
• Multiplication facts for practice and use in completing worksheets.
• Steps for things done in a sequence: problem solving, solving long division problems, observing and documenting an experiment, others.
• Assignments and due dates.

Bulletin Boards
Using Dinah Zike's *Foldables*™

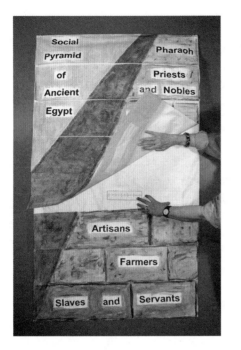
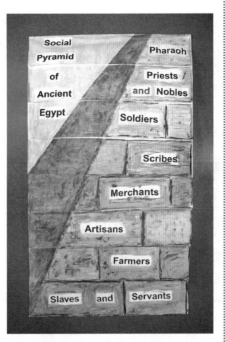

Layered Book

Use large sheets of bulletin board paper to make the giant Layered Books pictured on this page, or have fun designing your own. Remember, student work such as any of Dinah's *Foldables*™, quarter sheet and half-sheet publishing center pages, maps, diagrams, vocabulary words, internet print-outs of information, and much more, can be displayed under appropriate tabs of this large interactive bulletin board. See any book in Dinah Zike's *Big Book* series for instructions on how to make a Layered Book.

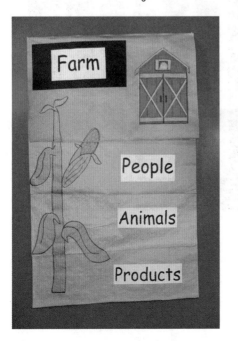

Bulletin Boards
Using Dinah Zike's *Foldables*™

Large Match Books

Use 8½" x 11" sheets of paper to make these large Match Books. Have fun designing your own. Remember, main ideas are represented on the front of the tabs, and supporting facts, definitions, pictures, answers to questions, and more can be written or glued under the appropriate tabs. (See any book in Dinah Zike's *Big Book* series for instructions on how to make and use Match Book *Foldables*™.)

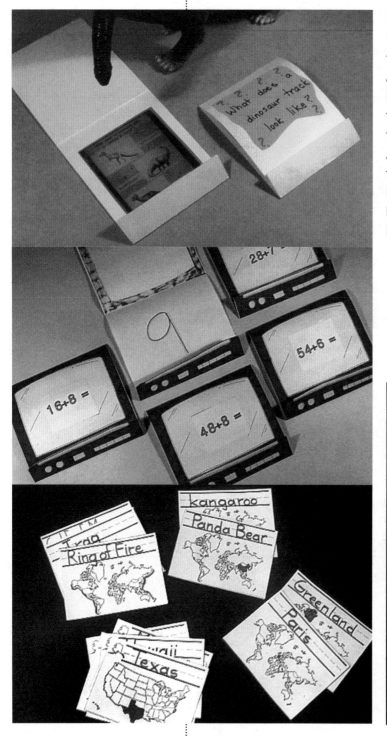

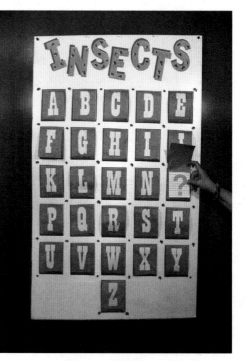

Bulletin Boards
Using Dinah Zike's *Foldables*™

Pyramid Mobile

Use 8½" x 11" sheets of paper or 12" x 18" sheets to make the large Pyramid Mobiles pictured. Have fun designing your own. Hang student work such as quarter-sheets of publishing center paper, labels, maps, diagrams, vocabulary words, and much more, from the appropriate sides of this 3-D display. (See any book in Dinah Zike's *Big Book* series for instructions on how to make a Pyramid Mobile.)

Bulletin Boards
Using Dinah Zike's *Foldables*™

Cube and Accordion *Foldables*™

Use large sheets of 12"x18" paper or sheets of poster board, to make the giant displays pictured. Have fun designing your own.

Remember, student work, such as any of Dinah's *Foldables*™, quarter-sheet and half-sheet Publishing

Center pages, maps, diagrams, vocabulary words, internet print-outs of information, photographs, magazine pictures, and much more, can be displayed on the sides of these interactive, folding bulletin boards. (See any book in Dinah Zike's *Big Book* series for instructions on how to make Accordion *Foldables*™ (like those above) and a Cube Foldable™ (below).

Bulletin Boards: 2" Tape

Taking Advantage of Tape

It is time to replace the bulletin board. You go to the file folder containing materials and letters for the next board. Upon opening the file you find numerous letters in a tangled stack. Looking at these letters makes it difficult to remember what the bulletin board looked like last year. As you play Scrabble® with the letters to form words, you discover that one or more of the letters is missing. Who knows what happens to them?

Now you must take time to find or make another letter. It is then you realize how much the other letters have faded. Cutting letters and putting letters up on a bulletin board one by one are time-consuming jobs.

Make letters for bulletin boards only once, and then assemble them into words using 2" clear tape. If needed, the words can be folded and stored perfectly in unit file folders and/or Unit Boxes (see page 157).

Bulletin Boards: Letters

Once Is Enough

Cut all letters for bulletin boards, labeling, and flash cards using 2" or 4" letter press patterns. These letters now fit perfectly on one or two strips of 2" clear tape to form words.

If the letters are to be mounted on another piece of paper, place them backwards and in reverse order on the clear tape so that they appear properly when taped to the background.

- To seal letters as words for use on a bulletin board, use tape on the front and back of the words. The word can then be stapled or tacked to a bulletin board.
- Bulletin board backgrounds show through the clear tape.
- If the board is covered with thin sheet of clear vinyl (page 33), the tape over the letters is not noticeable.

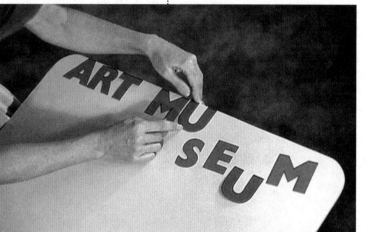

Other advantages of clear tape include:

- It is easier to align bulletin board words than a bunch of individual bulletin board letters.
- Mount words and titles quickly with push pins or staples: No more putting up individual letters one-at-a-time.
- Letters do not pull up around the edges when mounted.
- Less time is needed to assemble and display bulletin boards.

Bulletin Boards: Letters

Looking For Letters

Brightly-colored letters can be purchased at a teacher supply, art, craft, or scrapbook supply store. The letters pictured are 2 ½" tall. Once you have laid out the letters to form a word, place the 2" tape across the middle of these letters, forming words for the bulletin board. You can then turn the word over and "laminate" it with another 2" tape. This also covers the sticky areas between letters from the first tape.

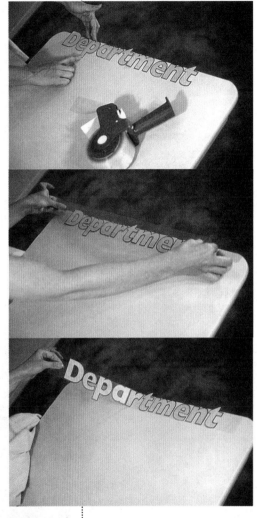

Letterpress Machines

Letterpress machines are now available on most school campuses, or within district educational service centers. These machines cut letters and shapes out of several layers of paper at a time. Try using the following types of paper when making letters for bulletin boards.

- Newspaper print
- Color advertising
- Construction paper
- Gift wrapping paper
- Aluminum foil
- Computer paper
- Old road maps
- Magazine pictures of specific objects (food, plant, animal, etc.)

Letter Files

Use a letter press to cut hundreds of upper and lower case 2" letters from the same kind and color of paper. Store letters in legal envelopes or resealable plastic sandwich bags, and file them in a long, narrow box. Leave this box of letters with your Classroom Helper (possibly a "Grandmother" or "Grandfather", see page 103), who will use tape to make words for bulletin boards as needed.

Bulletin Boards: Activities

*No! No! No!
Don't even think about it!
Tape has many practical
uses, but this is NOT one of
them!*

Giant Board Games

Clear tape can be used to mount pictures and words on backgrounds that cannot be laminated.

Example: Use long pieces of cardboard to make objective-based Twister® games for improving gross motor skills and reviewing basic information.

Tape pictures or words on the board. One student calls out the names of the pictures, and another student moves in response to the names called.

For a unit entitled "Mammals Around the World" the board (below) had small pictures of many different kinds of mammals. The caller might say "Left hand on a water buffalo, right foot on a rhino, left foot on a blue whale, right hand on an Bengal tiger."

Make the game even more challenging and fun! For example, say "Right hand on a mammal from Africa."

Walk Through The Textbook

Photocopy and greatly enlarge paragraphs, main ideas, or vocabulary words and definitions from the currently studied chapter of a textbook. Use 2" tape to adhere these pieces of information in sequential order from one end of a piece of cardboard to the opposite end. As a student reads the short chapter "blurbs" they move along the board. When finished, the student will have an overview of the key information in the chapter.

Preserving Specimens

Seal And Preserve Science Specimens

Use clear tape to adhere science specimens to a porous paper such as construction paper. The specimen will continue to dry through the porous paper after it is sealed on one side with tape, and will be preserved for years of classroom use.

Try It With These Specimens:

- Flowers
- Grasses and weeds
- Small dead insects
- Dead butterflies and moths
- Seeds
- Snake skin
- Leaves
- Root systems
- Insect wings and legs
- Soil samples
- Feathers
- Other delicate objects!

Jars can also be used to house specimens (below). Some specimen require filling the jar with a mothball or with rubbing alcohol in order to preserve them. For safety, hot glue the lid in place.

Clear tape and construction paper combine nicely when preserving science specimens. The specimens can be displayed in a variety of ways, and store easily for future use. Above, they are hung over a fabric bulletin board.

This photograph was taken in my office (left). I have found that storing specimens, such as feathers, fragile skulls, and large insects in jars prrotects them from humidity, mites, and other decompositional factors.

Displaying Student Work

Note From Dinah

Students appreciate having their academic accomplishments, artistic achievements, and other work displayed. At the beginning of the school year, it is usually easy to change and rotate student work. However, as the year progresses, and teachers become busier and busier, the task of changing these displays is often left to chance. Don't wait until papers begin to turn yellow to change out student work. Turn the task over to the students!

Museum Of Fine Work

Let students select the work they want to display. As graded papers are returned, or as artwork is completed, students can place new work in the "*Museum of Fine Work*" (next page) or in other displays discussed in this book.

Displaying Student Work

Museum Frames

Use small sections of corrugated or other thick cardboard, 10" x 12" or larger, as picture frames for displaying student art and academic work.

You can find pre-cut pieces of cardboard in boxes in which bottles are shipped, or buy them at boxing distributors (business phone directory). Use scissors or a hobby knife to cut single sheets of cardboard, or cut several sheets at a time with a jigsaw.

Making The Frames:

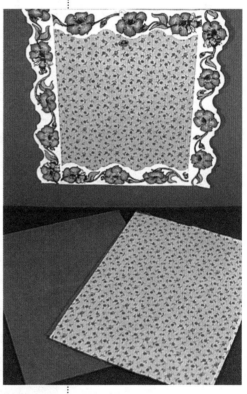

• Cut the thick or corrugated cardboard into uniform shapes larger than 8½" x 11".
• Paint the cardboard, or cover it with fabric or contact paper.
• Make a border for the frame by using colored tape, bulletin board borders, or strips of colored paper.
• Securely hang the frames on the wall. If the walls are made of cinder blocks, hang the picture frames against the wall using strings attached to the ceiling tiles (page 70). If your classroom has inadequate space for each child to have his own frame, use fewer frames and frequently rotate the student's work.
• Label the area "Museum of Fine Work."

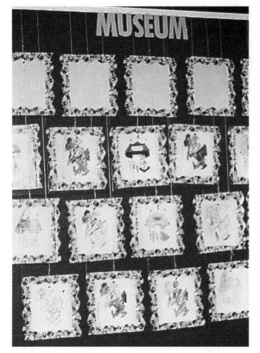

Hanging Bar

Screw cup hooks into a 1x2 or 1x4 wood board in a straight line, 2" apart. Attach the 1x2 horizontally to a wall, and hang your students' works. Notice how many rows can be hung from the hanging bar (left).

Displaying Student Work

Use clothespins and placemats to make a display area

Attach the clothespin to the placemat with a hot glue gun and wire. Punch a hole in the place mat on either side of the clothespin. Place a wire, such as a bag tie, through the back of the placemat, then through the spring in the center of the clothespin, and then through the other hole in the mat (illustration left). Twist together the wires behind the mat to hold the clothes pin in place.

Check Fire Codes

Check all applicable fire codes before hanging work from the ceiling.

Hanging The Mats

Hang the place mats using ribbon that has been stapled or hot glued to the mats.

Paper Ring Display

Cut a sheet of paper lengthwise into three strips. Glue both ends of each 11" strip together to form a ring. Cut 1" vertical slits on opposite sides of the ring. Slip vocabulary cards, sentence strips, etc. into the slots as shown.

Picture Frame Display

Make an inexpensive display aid by cutting a file folder in the shape of a "picture frame holder." You can use a real wood or plastic picture frame holder as a template.

Displaying Student Work

Resealable Bag Display

Use resealable plastic bags to make a student display board. Tape one gallon-size bags together with two-inch clear tape. Be careful not to tape over the resealable "zippers." In these photos we taped together fifteen bags, but you can tape together as many as you need. You can also try using smaller bags to display smaller work.

 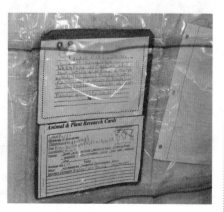

Displaying Student Work

Acetate sheet displays

Needed: Acetate sheets (8 1/2" x 11") and 2" clear tape.

1. Cut one acetate sheet into four 8½"-long strips.
2. Tape a strip of acetate to both the top and bottom of a full sheet of acetate (above). Do the same with the other two strips and another full sheet. This will make two display sections.
3. Attach the acetate display to a bulletin board by stapling or pinning them along the top edge (below).

This display is best used to show student work on notebook paper. Notebook paper is smaller than the 8½" x 11" acetate sheets used to make the display.

Displaying Student Work
Using Dinah Zike's *Foldables*™

Sentence Strip Holder Display

Use Dinah's *Sentence Strip Holder Foldables* for desks and bulletin boards. See page 13, or see any of the books in Dinah Zike's *Big Book* series for instructions and more ideas for their use.

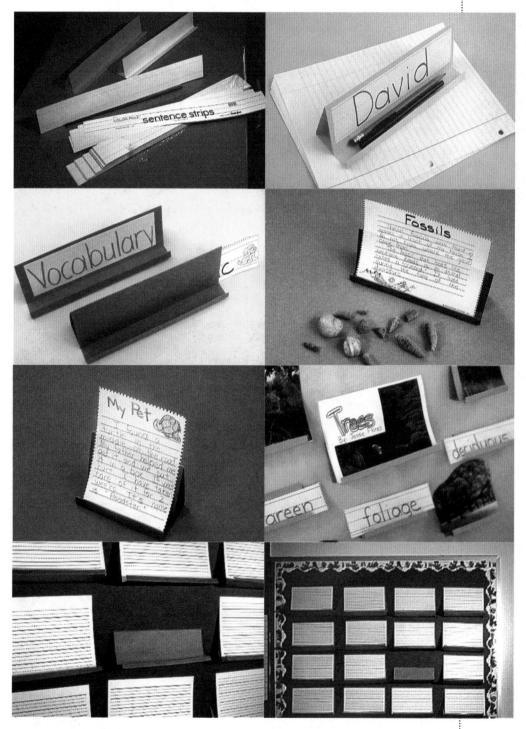

Classroom Storage

"Can Work"
Collect large or small coffee cans and paint them a bright color, or cover them with contact paper and decorate (see page 34).

Cheese Box Stack-Up
Paint processed cheese boxes (like Velveeta®) and use them for storage. These boxes stack well and fit into discovery or unit boxes. Use these boxes to hold flash cards, science specimens (leaves, bark, rocks, shells), checkers and game pieces, etc. With these boxes you can also make the "Lock 'Er Up" lockers described in the section on glue, page 17.

Bag It
Plastic resealable storage bags make excellent containers for science specimens (fossils, rocks, etc.), and for game and activity pieces. Use clear two-inch tape to attach a content label, or to attach an index card giving instructions on using the activity. Or, write directly on the bag with permanent markers, and cover the writing with 2" tape. This "laminates" the writing onto the bag.

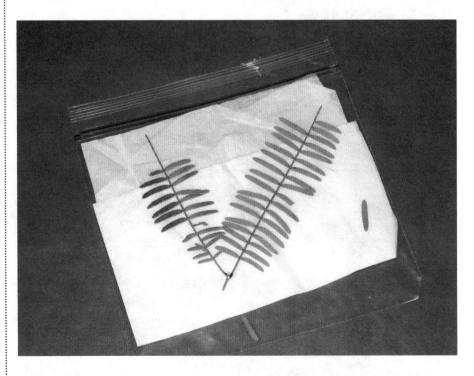

Classroom Storage

Clear Plastic Containers

Use clear plastic packaging containers from grocery stores and florists for storing and viewing specimens or fragile collectables. Seal containers using 2" clear tape.

before

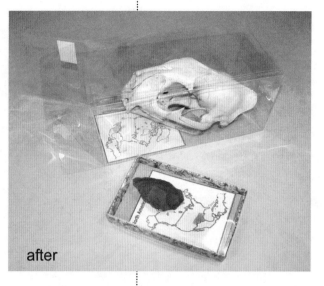

after

Stationery Boxes With Clear Lids

Use these boxes to display science specimens. Place a piece of soft or hard foam in the bottom of the container to hold or pin specimens. Greeting card boxes are more commonly available during the Christmas holiday season.

Food Containers

Clear plastic food containers found at deli's and used by restaurants as "to-go" containers make great display cases. Plastic containers with clear lids are used to serve cold lunches on many airlines. They are stacked and discarded after every flight.

Storage Boxes

As discussed throughout this book, boxes of varying sizes are ideal for sorting and storing. Use shoeboxes, gift boxes, large laundry detergent boxes with handles, cake mix boxes, and cereal boxes.

Classroom Storage

Butter Dishes And Plastic Containers
These throwaways hold a multitude of storage possibilities, and are easily collected from students and neighbors. (See the section on obtaining items for the classroom, page 98.)

Use these plastic containers for storing paints that are to be used with sponge brushes, extra crayons, paper clips, desk supplies, math manipulatives, and more.

Note From Dinah
Do not collect bird nests from trees, since they might be used by birds the next season. However, if a nest is found on the ground, or is obviously

abandoned, place it in a plastic container. Place the container in the freezer for 48 hours to kill any parasites or insects hidden in the nest, and then place the specimen in the classroom *Natural History Museum* (page 141) for observation.

Baby Food Jars
These small jars make excellent storage for various objects used in the classroom. They can be incorporated into games and classification activities. For example, a preschool teacher might have students:

- Sort buttons by color into the jars.
- Sort buttons by size into the jars.

If science specimens are stored in jars which are never to be opened, seal the lid onto the jar with hot glue or seal the lid with 2" tape.

Microwave Oven Dishes
Plastic trays from frozen TV dinners are perfect for separating objects for observation in a Learning Center. They can also be used when passing objects around the room for observation. (Place a magnifying glass on the dish with the object.)

Dishes with individual compartments can be used for sorting objects, or for compare and contrast activities.

Classroom Storage

Cake Mix Box Library

Collect numerous cake mix boxes. Cut off the lids. (See the section on obtaining materials for the classroom.)

Paint the boxes or cover them with contact paper or construction paper. When placed side by side, the boxes resemble library books.

If contact paper was used to cover the boxes, use a permanent marker to write on the end of the box to identify the activity held inside.

If a regular paper or paint was used to cover the box, place a strip of clear 2" tape across the end of the box, or across the "book" binding. Now the box can be labeled with overhead projector or dry-erase markers, and the label can be erased and changed as needed.

Place the boxes side by side on a shelf. Bookends will give the cake mix box library a finished touch.

Students can check out these activity "books" and take them to their desks or to a special place in the classroom.

Each box can be coded with colored circles on the binding, indicating the academic level of material in the box. Colored gummed circles, such as those used in some libraries, can be used for this purpose.

Use them for:
- Sentence strips
- Vocabulary words
- Spelling words and dictation sentences
- Math drill activities
- Small books to be read
- Objective-based games and matching activities
- Flash cards
- Half-sheets of writing paper

Classroom Storage

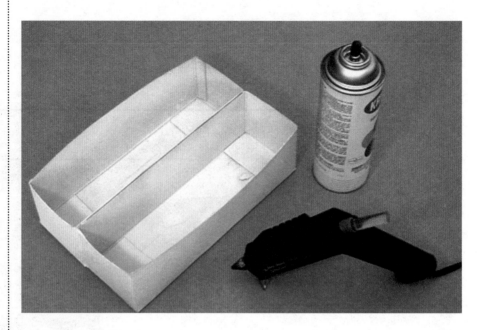

Mini Bookshelves

Use the bottom and top halves of a large cereal box to make mini book shelves. Cut the cereal box in half, and empty the contents into a storage container. Trim the ends so that the "shelves" are about 3 inches deep (above). Hot glue the "shelves" together and spray paint. Use them to hold Dinah Zike's *Mini Books* (below). See Dinah Zike's *Big Book of Phonics, Vocabulary, Spelling, and Grammar* for more ideas levels K-2 and 3-6.

Classroom Furniture

Stack It

Buy or make furniture that will stack. Use plastic Parsons tables or small wooden stools as seating and writing tables for young students. These make convenient reading circle chairs. Students can sit and read, then begin work in the circle by sitting on the floor and using the stools as tables. When not in use, they can be stacked and stored.

Remember, cardboard boxes can be painted, stacked, and glued and/or taped together with a strong, wide tape to form wall units for storage of lightweight objects.

This is a picture of a phonics station in my classroom when I taught first grade. Notice the stacked baskets, bins, and cushions. Students could sit on the floor and read to themselves, practice oral presentations, and/or watch the movement of their mouths as they blended sounds to form words.

I used stackable Parsons tables for my reading circle when working with kindergarteners and first graders. Students each sat on a table while in the reading group, and then sat on the floor and used their table as a work surface to start activity sheets or Foldables™ based on the day's reading skill.

Classroom Furniture

Household Furniture In The Classroom
Household furniture gives a classroom a comfortable, relaxed atmosphere. For ways to collect furniture, see the section on collecting materials for the classroom, beginning on page 98.

Bookshelves
Sectional bookshelves can be placed against the walls of a room, with each section becoming a different learning center or collection point for materials used in each subject. These are perfect for rooms with a lot of students and desks, but not much room for extended work areas or stations.

Here is a great idea that everyone uses because it works! Make inexpensive bookshelves with cinder blocks and 1" x 12" or 2" x 12" wood planks. Place this type of shelving against a wall, and anchor the wood planks to the wall. Do not trust them as free-standing shelves! They might fall. Never build shelves higher than three blocks high.

Bar Stool Table
A bar stool works well for the teacher during group instruction or "story time" and for students as a free-standing countertop to use as a science lab table. Bar stools are also perfect for small demonstration tables. The extra height enables all students to view the demonstration.

Study Areas
Couches, chairs, and coffee tables make comfortable reading areas and study spots to review and prepare for tests. They are also perfect for conferences with individual students and visiting parents. End tables and coffee tables make excellent *Check It Out!* areas or observation tables. They are lightweight, easily moved, and inexpensive. If you have hard floors, place felt or furniture guards on the leg tips of all furniture so it will slide easily without harming the floor.

Other Ideas:
• Children's plastic swimming pools make nice learning centers when cushions are added.
• Old kitchen service carts with rolling casters make efficient portable science labs, art supply tables, or publishing centers. I have seen teachers tie four or five pairs of scissors and four or five containers of glue to each end of a cart.
• A bar stool can be made out of a log stood on end. (Use this log to study tree development.)

Room Dividers

Room Dividers

Room dividers not only give your classroom a personal touch, but they also provide a setting for individualized instruction areas, computer centers, publishing centers, and private reading areas. In student work areas, I prefer room dividers that are transparent or translucent. I use opaque room dividers to hide messy supplies, stations, and storage areas.

Use blinds to make a room divider that can be opened, closed, raised, and lowered. When closed, the blind slats can be used as sentence strips. Write on the plastic or enameled blind slats with a dry erase or overhead projector marker, and erase with a damp cloth. Warning: this is messy. Only use this for writing that needs to be displayed for a long period of time or for the entire school year. For example, you might list the steps of the writing process, or rules for punctuation or phonics. If you do not want students to see the written information (for example during a test), open or raise the blinds.

Clear or decorated shower curtains, sheets, and drapes can be used as dividers. They can be tied to the side when not needed. Clip-on curtain hooks allow us to hang fabric and vinyl without sewing.

Stacked plastic baskets and crates can be used for room dividers, storage and furniture. (See page 133.)

Buy 1/2"- or 3/8"-thick, 4' x 8' or 2' x 8' sheets of insulation board and tie, tape, or hinge them together (below, left). Paint them or wrap them in fabric. (Use spray glue to attach the fabric to the boards.) They make great dividers (below, right) that are easy to fold and store when not in use.

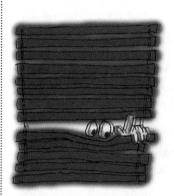

Check with home remodelers, interior decorators, and window coverings companies for used blinds and drapes that came out of homes that have been re-decorated.

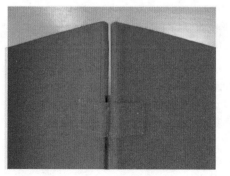 

These dividers do double duty as display boards. They are wrapped in felt in order to hang student work. Attach small strips of Velcro® (the "hook" strip only) to the back of work to be displayed. Press the work against the felt board, and the Velcro® hooks grab onto the felt!

Language Arts Notes & Ideas

Hallway reading nook, Boerne ISD, Boerne, TX

This light-weight, 1/4"-thick-foam-core board (art/craft supply stores) is perfect for collecting and displaying information on, articles about, or pictures of the featured author.

General Notes:

• I like students to work with partners for reading and spelling practice. This greatly increases the amount of time a student is reading aloud and silently.

• I would rather buy 3 books each of 10 different titles than buy 30 books of one title. Two students can read a book together, and I have a book to use to follow along. The third book can be used to replace a lost or damaged book.

• Inexpensive rugs, carpet scraps, sections of foam, or new pet beds are perfect for team reading areas.

• Timers can be used to keep teammates reading and on task equal amounts of time.

• Design "generic question" cards or worksheets so all students will be working on the same skill, no matter what story or book they are reading. For example, main idea cards and/or "ie" vocabulary word activities can be used with any story from any genre of literature.

• Move around and work with several teams during the team reading and spelling time. The next day, work with different teams.

• Take note of the author and/or illustrator of selections read in class, and feature beloved authors bi-weekly or more frequently if time permits.

• Use this board to generate expanded sentences. Place a noun (subject) and a verb (predicate) cards on the board, and ask students to make expanded sentences using the given words. For example, if the word cards are "dog" and "jumped", students might write:

The dog jumped.
The big, black dog jumped.
The big, black dog jumped into the car.

Repeat the activity with different word cards four days a week.

Language Arts Notes and Ideas

Vocabulary Activities

I like to group vocabulary words into the following categories: "Too Easy," "Too Hard," and "Just Right." I find students either already know "Too Easy" words or master them very quickly. The "Just Right" words are the ones we need to work on daily, and those who have mastered these are ready to move on to the "Too Hard" words. Kids love big words (like *Pachycephalosaurus*!) and enjoy the challenge.

Reading Activities

Have parents, guardians, grandparents, retirees, and famous people in your community read and record grade-level appropriate short stories or poems. Allow students to listen and read along.

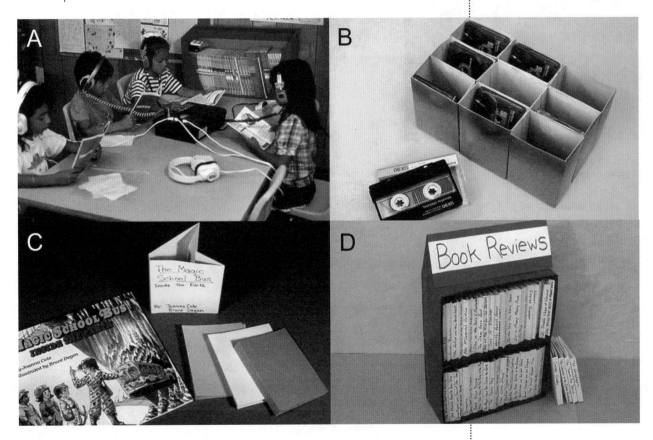

Other Activities

A. Students read silently as they listen to books on tape.

B. Tapes can be stored in small cereal boxes (see page 35).

C. Make mini book jackets to document and record impressions of books and stories read during the year.

D. Reviews can be stored in mini book cases (page 132). Students feel "smart" when they see how much they have read and when they discuss how the literature has enriched their lives.

Handwriting Table & Activity Center

This table could have been covered with a sheet of clear vinyl to increase its usefulness (see page 33).

Make A Unique Multipurpose Table—It's Easy

This homemade table serves as a supply station, an art center, and a handwriting practice area for beginning writers. (See Publishing Center chapter for ideas.)

How To Make It

This table (left) is easy to make and provides a wonderful place for kids to work! If I can build it, anybody can!.

Cut 1" x 4" boards and paint with enamel to represent pencils, markers, crayons or pens. Nail or screw 1 x 4's across the boards to make a solid frame. Make two of these frames to support the tabletop.

Use a piece of plywood, discarded door, or used countertop for the tabletop. Attach the supports to the tabletop, using steel angles or nails and glue.

The tablecloth is a pencil print fabric. The same fabric has been used to make a hanging fabric word chart.

Masonite Boards

Use the masonite chalkboards described on page 62 to practice handwriting skills.

Sidewalk Chalk Walk

Form the letter being studied using giant sidewalk chalk. Draw arrows to show the direction students are to walk to form the letter.

Write On The Table

Place a sheet of clear vinyl over the table and place handwriting practice sheets under the vinyl. Allow students to write on the table to practice handwriting skills (see page 33).

Art Center

Do Not Duplicate

If you have already designed a Supply Station and Publishing Center Station, you may not need to duplicate it by making an Art Center. Just add a box to store special art supplies such as paints and clay.

Which of these items do you need for your art center?

- Extra crayons
- Markers
- Small containers of glue
- A gallon of glue
- Pencils and pencil containers
- Erasers
- Paints and brushes
- Work aprons or shirts (optional)
- Paper (new and used)
- Hole punch
- Decorative scissors
- Yarn to make mobiles, and more!

Optional Work Aprons

Ask a parent, guardian, or classroom "grandparent" to make the work aprons pictured. Or, you can cut the arms off second-hand men's shirts and use them!

If you or a volunteer want to make them: • Cut an apron pattern out of paper, leaving an extra three inches at the bottom. Check the size of the pattern by comparing it to one of the students. Use the pattern to cut the apron out of the fabric. Hem all the edges. • To make pockets, turn up the bottom three inches, and sew both sides of the fold. Sew from the top of the fold to the bottom at two- to three-inch intervals. • Add cording to make the neck and ties. Make the ties long enough to wrap around the back and return to the front for easier tying by students.

When I was a young and energetic teacher first starting out, I made 20 copies of this blue apron (right) for my students!

Easels add verticle work space and yet can be folded for easy storage. Easels can often be found at garage sales and resale stores.

A teacher can't have too many pockets! The apron pictured below was a gift from Linette Liby, a fellow educator in Kansas. Look for blank aprons sold in craft stores, and customize your own.

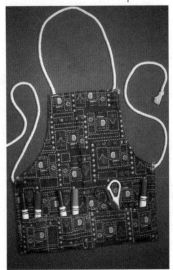

Science Lab

Supplying Your Science Lab

Which of these items do you need for your Science Lab?
- Magnifying glasses
- Microscope, if available
- Beakers, flasks, cylinders (available in plastic)
- One-minute and three-minute timers
- Storage containers and specimen collection containers: jars, small boxes, plastic bags, stationery boxes with clear lids, plastic containers and baskets, empty medicine bottles, film canisters, etc.
- Tongs for picking up objects
- Gloves (plastic and heavy fabric)
- Clear plastic measuring cups
- Measuring spoons
- Rubbing alcohol* for preserving specimens: large and small insects, small fish, reptiles, amphibians, & other small animals. Rule of Thumb for Using Alcohol: If the object is thicker than your thumb, use formaldehyde* or formalin.*
- Formalin* can be used with larger specimens.
- Flat trays or plates for passing objects and displaying.
- Rulers, yardsticks, meter sticks.
- Gram/ounce scales and/or balance scales.

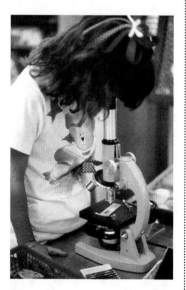

Large Jars

A one-gallon jar with a lid can be used for numerous things in a Science Center. Use it to conduct an experiment or to store and display fragile objects. One-gallon jars may be obtained at no cost from cafeterias or restaurants, or may be purchased in discount stores. One of the jar's most important uses will be to serve as a temporary habitat for unexpected animal visitors:

.....by adding water and plastic plants
.....by laying it on its side and adding sand or soil.
.....by laying it on its side and adding a small amount of water and rocks. Use clay as a base to keep it from rolling.
.....by placing wood shavings in the bottom.

Safe Return

Require students to return their animal friends to the same point of collection within 24 to 48 hours. Remind students NOT to collect living specimens they cannot return.

*Teacher use only. Keep out of reach of children. Know and follow your district's rules on toxic substances in the classroom.

Science Center vs. Natural History Museum

Is it a Science Center or is it a Museum

I can not tell you how many classrooms I have visited where the science center changes very little throughout the school year. There are rocks and minerals and feathers and nests on display, but they stay there the entire year! This is not a Science Center---it is a Natural History Museum.

A Science Center Is Constantly In Action

A Science Center is objective-based and relates to current units of study. It should constantly be in a state of change as new earth, life, and physical science topics are studied, new specimens are observed, and new experiments are performed. This is a good place to post the title of the current topic of study, list vocabulary words, display objects for observing and experiencing, and present a simple experiment that all students must complete before the end of the week..

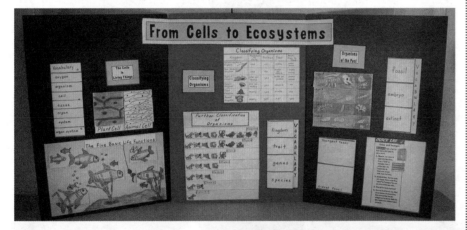

Details of a well-done display board (shown at upper left) for a Science Center.

A Natural History Museum is More Static

Leave a little shelf space for a Natural History Museum. Kids love observing specimens. Together as a class, determine how you will sort and organize the objects brought into the classroom.

Science Centers
Using Dinah Zike's *Foldables*™

Science Center Activities

Use these and other *Foldables*™ for science learning activities:

Specimen Display Boxes

4-Door Displays

Multi-part Pyramid Display

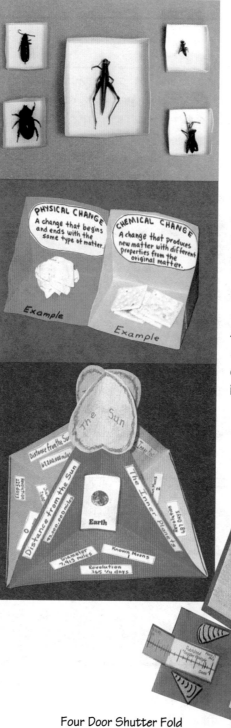

• Post current vocabulary terms.

• Display a periodic table of elements. Locate elements as they are discussed. For example, oxygen in the atmosphere, silicon in earth's crust, and calcium in bones.

• Use the *Foldables*™ below to display science specimens, make science work stations, and present science projects.

See Dinah Zike's *Big Book of Science: Elementary* and Dinah Zike's *Big Book of Science: Middle School/High School* for other ideas on using *Foldables*™ in the science classroom.

Four Door Shutter Fold

Weather Station

Reading And Recording

Ask permission to set up a mini weather station on the school grounds. It can be as simple as a plastic rain gauge and thermometer, or as complex as your budget allows. The rain gauge to the right is also capable of recording wind speed and direction, as well as tallying total rainfall amounts.

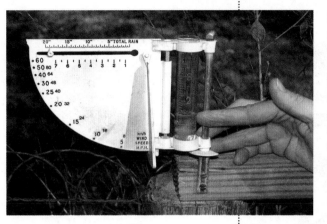

Place your rain gauge in an easy-to-reach location away from trees, shrubs, roofs, and anything else that can accidentally drip rainwater into the gauge.

Make multiple copies of the illustrations below and paste them onto a sheet of 8½" x 11" paper to make a master sheet. Use the illustrations in student journals, on bulletin boards, and in projects when reporting on precipitation and temperature.

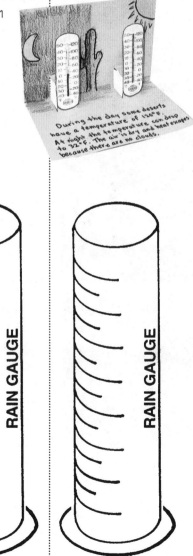

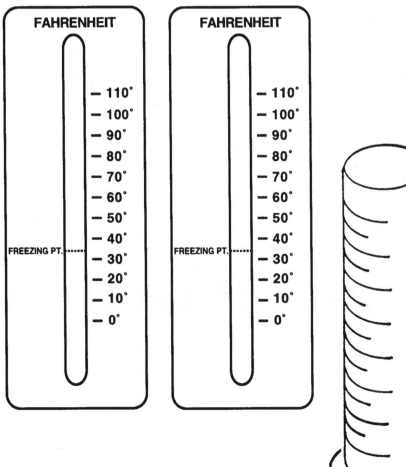

Library and Research Center

Heart And Soul

Books can become the heart and soul of the classroom – myths, magic, methods, models, and more. They must be present and easily accessible. As you collect materials for your room, ask for books – different kinds of books of different reading levels. (See page 95 on obtaining materials for the classroom.)

Students will begin to depend on these books to help them solve problems, discover new information, find role models, and explore worlds that differ from the one in which they live.

Start Your Collection:

Collect the following materials for your Library & Research Center. They can be in book or electronic form (CD, DVD, books-on-tape, etc).
- A set of general encyclopedias
- Reference books including appropriate higher-lead textbooks
- Picture encyclopedias
- Dictionaries
- Classic literature
- Poetry
- Picture books
- Short stories
- Biographies
- Cook books for kids
- Gardening information
- How-to books
- Repair books

Visiting Books

Use Dinah Zike's large *Foldable*,™ the *4-door Display** (bottom left) to feature "Visiting Books" or books brought to school by students. Try to read, or at least skim through, all books before placing them on display. I have been shocked by the content found in a few books written for elementary readers. Do not take it for granted that a book will be appropriate for your community of students and parents just because it is written on a certain reading level.

*See any of Dinah Zike's Big Book series for this and other *Foldables*™ ideas and activities for your classroom.

Library Organization

Dot-To-Dot

For very young students, place colored dots on the spines of books (these are found in office supply stores) to color code your classroom library books. I use green dots to indicate science books, blue dots for social science books, orange dots for math books, red dots for fictional story books, yellow dots for fairy tales and nursery rhymes, etc. The library helper places books on the shelves by matching the colored dots.

Dewey Decimal*

Use a generic version of the Dewey Decimal system to organize your library. Place dots on book spines, and write numbers 0-10 on the dot depending on the area of the library in which the book would be found. Use the chart in the photo below to help you begin this process of organization.

Bibliography Form

Photocopy this form several times. Tape or glue copies onto one sheet of paper, and make numerous copies of this paper. Allow students to use this form when giving credit to a source when writing a paper or reporting on a book they have read.

Study Topic: _____
Reference Sources: _____
Publication: _____
Author: _____
Copyright: _____

*For more informatiion on library skills and language arts skills, see Dinah Zike's *Big Book of Word Lists: Phonics, Spelling, Vocabulary, and Grammar.*

Map & Globe Center

Every Classroom Needs One
Every classroom needs a Map and Globe Center, or at the very least a good atlas and/or a globe. Geography and social studies should be continuously integrated into the curriculum!

Geographic Knowledge Enhances The Reading Experience
A knowledge of world geography can be obtained while studying the different earth, life, and physical sciences. Science classes and labs must have easy access to world and regional maps.

As a class reads a story about a koala, they should be able to find the region of the world in which this animal lives. A basic knowledge of geography adds to reading comprehension and appreciation.

Where In The World?
Abbreviations and capitalization are studied in language arts classes. Use the Map and Globe Center as an aid in teaching these skills. The etymology of words is incorporated easily into language and spelling classes: "Where in the world did the origin of this word begin?"

Current Events
Discuss current events using a map and globe. Encourage parents to keep a globe near the television, and as their child hears interesting information about another part of the world, help them find the area. (This also helps improve parents' and teachers' geography skills as well.)

Note From Dinah
Use sticky-back notes to mark and label locations on your maps and globes. Remove labels as students become familiar with locations, and add new ones as needed.

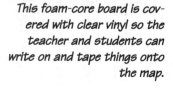

This foam-core board is covered with clear vinyl so the teacher and students can write on and tape things onto the map.

Social Studies Current Events
Using Dinah Zike's Foldables™

Current Events Framed

Use large, laminated picture frames to feature articles relating to local, state, national and world news events. Articles can be taped to the frames and removed to make way for the next newsworthy articles. Use one of the class charts on page 79 to keep track of who has and who has not contributed an article to the weekly board.

Make matchbook Foldables™ to collect and display current event articles and pictures. Small maps can be glued to the front to show the location of the event.

Store matchbook Foldables™ in a small plastic container and place it in your social studies center next to a globe of the world.

Collect current event articles and pictures from newspapers, magazines, and the Internet, and place them on the Current Events board. Change the articles as students bring in new ones. Remind students to look for and collect articles that interest them.

Current Events Quilt

Use a paper cutter to cut scratch paper into 8½" squares. Have students bring current event articles from home (or use classroom newspapers). The student bringing the article reads the entire article, summarizes it orally to the class, and then cuts out the first six or more paragraphs or paragraph clusters that summarized the key points. This condensed article is glued onto an 8½" square and mounted on the wall to gradually form a big current events quilt.

These pictures are from my classroom when I taught first grade at Anderson-Shiro ISD, Anderson, Texas. Most of my collection of photographs of my former classrooms were destroyed in a flood.

Social Studies
Using Dinah Zike's *Foldables*™

Classroom Tips
- Post current social studies vocabulary
- Feature key people, past and present, by doing Who, What, When, and Where activities
- Feature key locations and events by doing What, When, Where, and Why/How activities
- Make sure you have access to good maps and/or a globe.

Timelines
I am constantly surprised to learn how many students in the public school system do not have an understanding of the chronological order of key events in the history of their community, state, nation, and the world. And yet, I have seen first graders in Montesorri schools who know that trains were used as transportation before automobiles and after caravels. Timelines are an integral part of every classroom in a Montesorri program; yet they are used in a random fashion in the public schools. I believe in timelines, and I have invented several ways in which they can be easily made and stored.

See any of the books in Dinah Zike's *Big Book* series for instructions on how to make the timelines featured in this book (see page 56), and for hundreds of ideas for using *Foldables*™ to teach social sciences:
  - Dinah Zike's *Big Book of Social Studies: Elementary*
  - Dinah Zike's *Big Book of United States History: Grades 5-12*
  - Dinah Zike's *Big Book of World History: Grades 6-12*

This was the culminating activity for our study of Japan (above). Note the maps on the wall. We were attempting to eat rice using chop sticks. I was fortunate to have a parent who often purchased items for the classroom and/or the students that enhanced our studies. The hats and fans pictured were purchased from the Oriental Trading Company. They have a wonderful website at www.orientaltrading.com or you can call 800-875-8480.

Display Artifacts and Projects
Use any of Dinah Zike's display *Foldables*™ to organize and feature materials to enhance your social studies curriculum.

Math Center

Math Center Activities

• Post current vocabulary terms in the math center.
• Try to do a word problem every day that reinforces the skills being studied.
• Make and use circle graphs, bar graphs, and line graphs when teaching math, science, and social studies. Try to do at least one graph a week.
• Make and use tables and charts to record math information.
• Frequently practice writing and reading whole numbers and rational numbers to reinforce place value.
• Use grid chart paper.
• Provide and frequently use linear, liquid, and mass measurement tools.
• Display a negative number line displaying positive and negative integers

The hundreds grid pictured above was made using small condiment cups hot-glued to a piece of foam core.

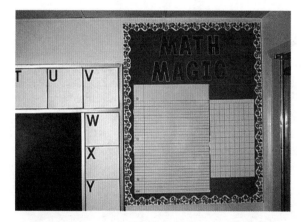

The laminated blank paper seen in this math center can be used to record changing terms and concepts being studied.

Short sentence strip holders of different colors can be used to display place value cards (see page 13).

Measurement Center

Measurement Activities
• Cut classroom sets of plastic cording, (right) found in craft stores, into the following lengths:
- one foot.
- one yard.
- one meter.

Use them to measure items in and out of the classroom.

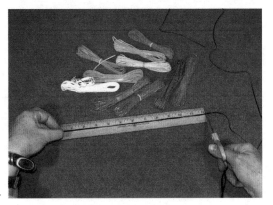

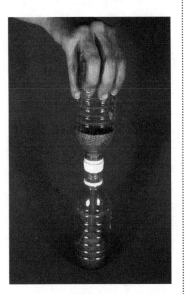

This class-made timer was made using two water bottles. A hole was drilled through one cap, and the other cap was discarded. Dyed cornmeal was placed inside one bottle, and before taping the bottles together they were held in position and turned. This allowed the cornmeal to flow from one bottle to the other so it could be determined (calibrated) how much cornmeal was needed to measure one minute or three minutes, etc. Extra cornmeal is discarded and the bottles are taped together. (From Dinah Zike's Big Book of Books and activities.)

• Use clocks and timers. The class-made timer (left) was made using two water bottles with a 1/4" hole drilled in one cap (discard the second cap), corn meal dyed blue (using rubbing alcohol mixed with food coloring), and 2" tape connecting the two bottles at the neck. Before taping the bottles together, use a stopwatch or minute hand to calibrate the amount of corn meal needed to pass through the hole in one minute. Discard extra cornmeal. Test the timer once more to make sure it is accurately measuring one minute before taping the bottles together.

• Use stop watches to record time, and to record how long events take when reporting science observations.

• Use Dinah Zike's Layered Books to make the following measurement aids to be used frequently to reinforce measurement and equivalencies:
Linear Measurement
Time Measurement
Liquid Measurement
Weight Measurement

• Practice telling time using analog and digital clocks.

• Use cylinders, beakers, flasks, and other measurement tools.

• Collect and use scales and other measurement tools.

• For more activities see Dinah Zike's **Big Book of Books and Activities** and **Big Book of Math, Elementary.**

Computer Center

Ideas For Your Computer Center

• Obtain as many computers and printers as possible for your classroom. Consider placing an ad in a local paper or let your neighbors know that you need old, but reliable computers.

• Try using stacks of smooth (unbent) scratch paper in your printer. The clean, backside of this previously used paper is perfect for printing reference articles or other materials used for research. If this works with your printer, it will save a lot of paper.

• Staple computer-generated reference materials inside shutter folds, as illustrated, to make reference "books" for your classroom.

Make a bibliography label that can be filled in and applied to each folder to give credit to the reference sources (see page 145 for reproducible).

• Use encyclopedias and other reference materials on disk. Print needed articles, staple them inside shutter folds as illustrated, and allow students to use these reference materials for projects and reports.

• Use the computer to conduct primary source interviews. As a class, communicate with people via email who are experts in topics you are studying. Again, remind students not to give personal information to anyone. Always use the school email address, and keep conversation strictly professional, not personal.

First Aid Center

This Health Center sign is thirty inches long and made with poster board to resemble a huge adhesive bandage. A real adhesive bandage was glued to the center.

What a Quack

It is amazing what a wet paper towel will "cure" in a classroom.

In classrooms that do not have sinks or water available, students must leave the room to get a wet paper towel to cure their headaches, stomach aches, or swelling bump.

In the first aid center, have paper towels available and a spray container filled with distilled water freshened with a couple of drops of lemon extract or a drop of lemon oil.

Pillow Power

Small pillows that students can take to their desks for resting their heads often expedite recovery from minor incidents, or aid those students who are feeling ill. Always have students cover pillows with paper towels before using, and wash pillows frequently.
Note: This is not an option in schools where head lice are a problem.

Possible Supplies For This Center:
- Small pillows
- Paper towels
- Spray container of distilled water
- Facial tissues
- Mirror
- Hand soap
- Paper Cups
- Toothpaste and toothbrushes (when studying dental hygiene, if appropriate)

NOTE: The Health Center Helper (page 44) is responsible for keeping the First Aid Center clean.

Setting Up A Classroom

Before and After

AFTER

Here we added a wall dictionary, bulletin boards, chalkboard tray displays, and grouped the desks to form tables.

We designated the right side of the blackboard as the Math Center. Shelves were made from cinder blocks and 1 x 12 boards. Math manipulatives were stored on the shelves and current math vocabulary words were written on the bulletin board.

AFTER

BEFORE

Setting Up a Classroom

Before and After

Here we set up a Science Center book shelf and display area. We covered the wall with giftwrap paper to protect the wall from experiments and to create an inviting nook for study .

AFTER

BEFORE

We placed a steel cabinet perpendicular to the wall to divide the space into two areas. The bookcases were found in a thrift shop and cleaned up and given a fresh coat of enamel paint.

AFTER

Setting Up a Classroom

Before and After

AFTER

BEFORE

Here we created a Publishing Center and Library. The wire book rack was found behind a book store in a dumpster.

AFTER

This area was used for classroom organization. It includes a Helper's Wheel and a work display bulletin board.

BEFORE

Setting Up a Classroom

Before and After

BEFORE

AFTER

Here and below we used 4' x 8' corrugated plastic sheeets to make giant display boards. Look under "Plastic Supply or Distributors" in your business phone directory.

BEFORE

AFTER

It seemed to take hours to adjust the student desks to the same height, but it was worth the effort.

Unit Boxes

Organize And Store All Your Stuff

One of the biggest problems facing teachers is organizing and storing the vast amount of materials needed to teach many subjects on different academic levels. Think of how long it takes to gather and organize all of the materials needed to teach a new unit. Bulletin board materials are stacked in a drawer or in a file cabinet, or rolled and stored on a shelf. Worksheets and activities must be pulled from numerous areas. Physical objects must be collected and prepared for display. Books and visual aids need to be checked and reviewed, etc.

Getting Started

Think of organizing all of your materials into Unit or Skill Boxes. Unit Boxes might include the following:

• A file folder containing...
> ...a unit plan.
> ...master copies of all activity sheets and worksheets.
> ...master copies of all evaluation procedures used.

• Bulletin board words and vocabulary words that have been put together with clear tape.
• Bulletin board pictures and maps, folded. Since the board will be covered with clear vinyl, laminating is unnecessary. If materials are already laminated, cut them into sections and hinge them with clear tape. Fold and store them in the Unit Box.
• Visual aids for activities and demonstrations. Make these out of a foldable material or out of posters small enough to fit in the box. Vinyl, fabric, plastic, and oil cloth can be used.
• Flash cards and activities.
• Specimens and any physical objects needed for observation.
• *Foldables*™ and other manipulatives.
• Books and magazines relevant to the unit.
• Puzzles or games that reinforce objectives.
• Poems, plays, songs, puppets, etc.
• Cards used for grouping activities (see pages 80, 81).

Unit Boxes

One Box For Each Unit

For some units, two boxes may be needed for your materials; however, you will be surprised how much will fit into one box when the unit is carefully planned. This will also help to pare down all your "stuff" to just the essentials. Remember, a good unit plan is an important component of Unit Box organization.

It All Stacks Up

Stack the boxes along a wall of your room (check local fire codes), or keep them at home or in the attic or garage. If you can, have only the boxes you need at school at any given time.

Uniformity Is The Key

Cardboard boxes of uniform size make ideal stackables. Ask companies that use copy machines to save their paper boxes. Check with print shops for extra boxes. It also is possible to buy boxes that are very sturdy and of uniform size from moving companies and box distributors. (Check your local business telephone directory.)

Boxes Can Be Beautiful

If desired, paint the boxes with latex enamel paint, or cover them with contact paper. Use 2" letters and clear tape to label the ends. Allow students to bring stickers or create original art with which to decorate the boxes.

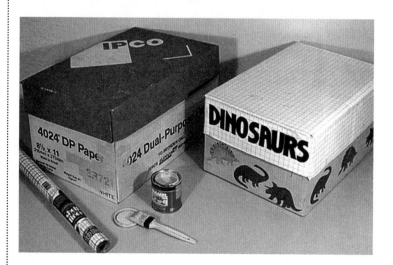

Unit Boxes

Unit Plan Forms

If you Teach using the "Unit Method," it might be helpful for you to design your own unit plan form. These are topics you might want to consider including in your form:

• Objectives to be taught.
• Introductory activities to generate interest.
• Multi-disciplinary activities to teach skills and objectives.
• Evaluation procedures to be implemented.
• Culminating activities to close the unit of study.
• Books and audio-visual materials for reference.
• Bulletin board layouts, sketched as memory aids for next year.
• Floor plan for Learning Center or work stations used for the unit.

Set Your Goals

By making just two or three Unit Boxes each semester, you will soon see how much time and energy you have saved. Four to six new Unit Boxes each year would be a major accomplishment.

Index

Activity Center, Handwriting Tablet 138
Art Center 139
Assessment: Averaging Grades 76
Assessment Documentation 77
Assessment In General 76
Assessment of Portfolios 73
Bulletin Boards 114
Bulletin Boards Using Dinah Zike's *Foldables*™ 113
Bulletin Board Letters 118
Bulletin Boards, Shaped 109
Bulletin Boards, Using 107
Bulletin Boards, Permanent 108
Bulletin Boards, Taping 120
Calendar Reproducible 54
Cereal Box Storage 35
Check It Out! 86
Collect Effectively 98
Computer Center 151
Computer Lists 79
Classroom Furniture 133
Classroom Jobs 39
Classroom, Setting Up 153
Classroom Storage 128
Classroom Work Baskets 68
Communicating & Networking 97
Crayons 22
Crayons, Giant 24
Cubicles & Display 112
Current Events/Social Studies Using Dinah Zike's *Foldables*™ 147
Displaying Student Work 122
Displays, Cubicles 112
Displays For Student Work Using Dinah Zike's *Foldables*™ 126
Everyone Works & Shares 93
File Folders: Assessment & Storage 75
First Aid Center 152
Fold-away Teaching Aids 105
Foldables™ Examples
  Accordion Fold 116
  Bound Book 145, 72
  Display Case 142, 148
  Four-Door Book 50,
  Four-Door Diorama 142, 144, 148
  Four-Tab Book 141

Index

Layered-Look Book 27, 113, 141
Match Book 114, 147
Pocket Book 67
Pop-Up Book 143
Pyramid Fold 106
Pyramid Fold Diorama 59, 142
Pyramid Fold Mobile 70, 115
Sentence Strip Holder 13, 127, 136, 149, 155, 156
Shutterfold 56, 151
Standing Cube 106, 116
Three Pocket Book 67
Three-Tab Book 141
Two-Tab Book 141, 56
Fleamarkets & Garage Sales 99
Furniture, Classroom 133
Garage Sales & Fleamarkets 99
Giant Crayons 24
Glue 14 - 19
Grades 71
Grouping Activities 80
Handwriting Table & Activity Center 138
Handwriting Tablets & Notebook Paper 47
Hanging Student Work 70
Help, Getting It 102
Helper's Wheel 40
Helper's Wheel Reproducibles 55
Home Survey 95
Home Survey Form 96
Hundreds Grid Reproducible 54
Job Descriptions & Training 42
Jobs, Classroom 39
Junk Box Art & Stress Release 94
Language Arts Notes & Ideas 136
Library & Research Center 144
Library Organization 145
Lining Up 84
Magnetic Boxes 64
Map & Globe Center 146
Maps, U.S., & World Reproducibles 52
Markers 30
Math Center 149
Measurement Center 150
Natural History Museum 141

Index

Neighborhood Scavenger Hunt 101
Networking & Communicating 97
Notebook Paper & Handwriting Tablets 47
Overhead Projector Markers 31
Paints 28
Paper 48
Pass It Around 90
Pencils 9
Pens 13
Photographs For Identity 38
Picture Frames 50
Picture Frame Reproducibles 51
Portfolios: Assessment & Storage 73
Pledge To The Flag 45
Preserving Specimens 121
Publishing Center 48-52
    Rubber Stamps & Punches 61
    Scratch Paper 58
    Templates 60
Quarter Sheets & Picture Frames 50
Quarter Sheet Reproducible 51
Rain Gauge Reproducible 143
Recording Grades 72
Reproducibles:
    Calendar 54
    Helper's Wheel 55
    Hundreds Grid 54
    Quarter Sheet 54
    Rain Gauge 143
    Timeline 53
    Thermometer 143
    U.S. Map 52
    World Map 52
Room Dividers 135
Rubber Stamps & Punches 61
Scavenger Hunt, Neighborhood 101
Science Centers Using Dinah Zike's *Foldables*™ 142
Science Lab 140
Scissors 20, 21
Scratch Paper 59
Show & Share 85
Social Studies/Current Events Using Dinah Zike's *Foldables*™ 147
Social Studies Using Dinah Zike's *Foldables*™ 148

Index

Storage, Classroom 128
Storage, Cereal Box 35
Storing Supplies 34
Student Response Boards 62
Student Work, Displaying 122
Student Work, Hanging 70
Study Cards & Flash Cards 65
Supplies8
Supplies, Storing 34
Take A Look At This! 91
Thematic Unit Plan Sheets 160
Thermometer Reproducibles 143
Templates 60
Timeline Reproducibles 53
Trash 36
Unit Boxes 157
Want Ads 100
Water Colors 27
Weather Station 143
Work Baskets 68
Write Here, On The Table 33
Writing A Little A Lot 49

Notes

Notes

Notes

Notes

Notes